Dialogical Argumentation and Reasoning in Elementary Science Classrooms

New Directions in Mathematics and Science Education

Series Editors

Wolff-Michael Roth (*University of Victoria, Canada*)
Lieven Verschaffel (*University of Leuven, Belgium*)

Editorial Board

Angie Calabrese-Barton (*Michigan State University, USA*)
Pauline Chinn (*University of Hawaii, USA*)
Lyn English (*Queensland University of Technology*)
Brian Greer (*Portland State University, USA*)
Terezinha Nunes (*University of Oxford, UK*)
Peter Taylor (*Curtin University, Perth, Australia*)
Dina Tirosh (*Tel Aviv University, Israel*)
Manuela Welzel (*University of Education, Heidelberg, Germany*)

VOLUME 34

The titles published in this series are listed at *brill.com/ndms*

Dialogical Argumentation and Reasoning in Elementary Science Classrooms

By

Mijung Kim and Wolff-Michael Roth

BRILL
SENSE

LEIDEN | BOSTON

All chapters in this book have undergone peer review.

The Library of Congress Cataloging-in-Publication Data is available online at http://catalog.loc.gov

ISSN 2352-7234
ISBN 978-90-04-39255-7 (paperback)
ISBN 978-90-04-39256-4 (hardback)
ISBN 978-90-04-39257-1 (e-book)

Copyright 2019 by Koninklijke Brill NV, Leiden, The Netherlands.
Koninklijke Brill NV incorporates the imprints Brill, Brill Hes & De Graaf, Brill Nijhoff, Brill Rodopi, Brill Sense, Hotei Publishing, mentis Verlag, Verlag Ferdinand Schöningh and Wilhelm Fink Verlag.
All rights reserved. No part of this publication may be reproduced, translated, stored in a retrieval system, or transmitted in any form or by any means, electronic, mechanical, photocopying, recording or otherwise, without prior written permission from the publisher.
Authorization to photocopy items for internal or personal use is granted by Koninklijke Brill NV provided that the appropriate fees are paid directly to The Copyright Clearance Center, 222 Rosewood Drive, Suite 910, Danvers, MA 01923, USA. Fees are subject to change.

This book is printed on acid-free paper and produced in a sustainable manner.

Contents

Preface	vii
List of Figures and Tables	ix

1 Argumentation Research in Science Education — 1
  Toulmin Argument Patterns — 3
  Dialogue and Presumptive Argumentation — 6
  Scientific Reasoning through Argumentation — 8
  Overview — 10

2 Vygotsky's Spinozist Perspectives on Language — 15
  The Real Life of Language — 17
  From Meaning to Sense — 23
    The Sense-giving Contexture — 23
    The Lived World Indicated by the Sign — 24
    The System of Signs — 29
    Sign-use as an Expressive Act — 30
    Sign-use as a Communicative Act — 31
    The Communicative Act as Soliciting a Behavior — 32
    The In-order-to Motive and the *Now, Here,* and *Thus* of the Communicative Act — 33

3 Children's Reasoning and Problem Solving — 37
  The Complexity of Young Children's Reasoning — 38
  What is Evidence? — 44
  Evidence in Nested Sense-giving Contexture — 50

4 Argumentation as Joint Action — 57
  The Social Nature of the Word — 57
  Argumentation and Emergence — 59
  Laying the Garden Path in Walking — 64
  Individualizing Collective Claims and Evidence — 67
  Resolution of Contradictions and Emergence of New Trouble — 73
  The Social Nature of Argumentation — 76

5 The Role of Physical Objects in Science Lessons — 79
The Commonness and Difference of Physical Objects — 80
Abstraction: What is Happening in the Real Event? — 85
Physical Objects that Contribute to the Making of Sense — 87
Learning with Physical Objects — 89

6 Argumentation and Inscriptions — 91
A Lesson Fragment — 92
From Explaining an Observation to Warranting a Claim — 96
Inscriptions in the Establishment of a Warrant — 98
Opportunities Arising from Working on the Chalkboard — 103

7 Argumentation and the Thinking Body — 107
Position and Disposition — 109
Thinking and Speech — 115
Unity/Identity of Body and Mind — 118
On Overcoming the Psychophysical Problem — 122

8 Teaching Argumentation in Elementary Science — 125
Attending to the Physicality of Argumentation — 127
Pointing and Formulating — 129
Being a Member of a Problem-Solving Community — 132

Index — 137

Preface

Science educators have come to recognize children's critical thinking and problem solving skills as crucial ingredients of scientific literacy. As a consequence, there has been a widespread, concurrent emphasis on argumentation as a way of developing critical and creative minds. Argumentation has been of increasing interest in the field of science education as a means of actively involving students in science and, thereby, as a means of promoting their learning, reasoning, and problem solving. However, many approaches to teaching argumentation place primacy on teaching the structure of the argumentative genre prior to and at the beginning of participating in argumentation. According to pragmatist philosophers of language, however, such an approach is absolutely impossible because to be able to learn the structure of argumentation, one already needs to be competent in argumentation in the same way that learning grammar requires knowing the language.

In this book, we offer a different approach based on dialogical relations, as the origin of internal dialogue (inner speech) and higher psychological functions. We follow scholars from very different disciplines—philosophers (e.g. G. H. Mead, K. Marx and F. Engels, E. V. Il'enkov), psychologists (L. S. Vygotsky, A. N. Leont'ev), and sociologists (e.g. H. Garfinkel, E. Livingston)—who have shown that there is a primacy of the social relations over mind. In this approach, argumentation first exists *as* dialogical relation for participants who are *in* a dialogical relation with others and who employ argumentation *for* the purpose of the dialogical relation. Using data from elementary school children's conversations in science classrooms, we describe and explain how argumentation emerges and develops *as, in,* and *for* dialogical relations with others. This sets the stage for argumentation to show up some time later when students are tested individually. For teachers the movement is in the reverse, for something known individually may unfold distributed over two or more people (e.g. teacher and student). The later Vygotsky adopted a Marxian Spinozist orientation toward knowing, learning, and development, an orientation that was elaborated in particular by the philosopher E. V. Il'enkov. The Spinozist position allows us to overcome the intellectualization of scientific argumentation and scientific literacy.

In this book, we contextualize our work by examining the current practice of teaching and researching children's argumentation and reasoning in elementary science classrooms such as the argumentation patterns that the philosopher of science S. Toulmin described or the argumentation schemes that derive from the work of D. Walton, and other various approaches in science education research. The approach to understanding and teaching classroom argumentation in this book is different from these existing studies. Much of the existing work on argumentation in science investigates older students. In contrast, we use empirical data from elementary classrooms to explain how argumentation emerges and develops in and from classroom interactions by focusing on think*ing* and reason*ing* through/in relations with others. We thereby also exemplify that it is possible to engage young children in argumentation prior to their understanding its structure—just as these same children do a lot of grammatically correct talking without yet knowing formal grammar. We have chosen to take this route because of independently articulated claims that dialogue is the first instantiation of a new form of language, which sets up the theoretical ground for this book.

We acknowledge the support we received from different grants. Mijung Kim collected data with a grant from the CER-Net Research and IRG-SSHRC General Research Grant at the University of Victoria. Her initial research was continued with a grant (to Wolff-Michael Roth) from the Social Sciences and Humanities Research Council of Canada (#435-2013-0260). We also draw on data obtained through grants #410-93-1127 and M-812-93-0006 (awarded to Roth). In chapter 3, we draw on materials originally published in Kim, M. and Roth, W.-M. (2017), Dialogic argumentation in elementary science classrooms. *Cultural Studies in Science Education.*

We thank the schoolteacher and students who participated in this study for sharing their enthusiasm, creativity, and open minds with us to make this work possible. Being and working with them in their classroom was truly inspiring and enlightening. We thank them for this wonderful journey together.

Figures and Tables

FIGURES

1.1.	The structure of an argument according to Toulmin (1958/2003).	4
2.1.	This revised transcription of Fragment 2.1 includes the simultaneous actions of the recipients resulting in an inherently social *transaction* of *corresponding*. The reply arises in and from attending and receiving speech, which together constitute the phenomenon of *responding*. It, too, is a transaction and thus social through and through.	18
2.2.	The drawing allows different figure–ground constellations. Depending on how you gaze, the dominant figure may be a white Maltese cross or a black cross along the diagonals. Some may also see something like a square circus tent viewed from above.	24
2.3.	A scene from an elementary classroom where 20 students are engaged in a tug of war against their science teacher (in doorway), who had "rigged" the competition in his favor using a block and tackle. The inclination of the students' bodies give a sense of the effort they make to win against their teacher.	25
2.4.	A scene from the whole-class discussion where the students and teacher are engaged in an argumentation about why the 20 students had lost the tug of war. Here, Shamir presents the design of a competition that he proposes would no longer favor the teacher.	26
3.1.	Introducing the mystery object.	39
3.2.	Observing and discussing in a small group.	42
3.3.	Observing the mystery object and onion together.	49
4.1.	This artistic rendering of a mixed second- and third-grade classroom shows how the students sit along an approximate arc at one end of which the teacher (right) is situated.	59
4.2.	This artistic rendering shows the children and the teaching assistant gathered around a water jar in which their pieces of carrot float. The children are asked to generate hypotheses about what makes the carrot float in the water to which salt has been added.	61

4.3.	The two articulations of the same phrase exhibit different intonations, which distinguishes the functions of the phrases the conversation. The dictionary sense ("meaning") of the phrases is the same: salt is making the carrot heavier.	69
5.1.	Physical abstraction in the event.	87
6.1.	At the end of the whole-class discussion, the chalkboard was littered with drawings that the teacher or students drew while talking the design of a pulley system to be used in a tug of war. Some drawings were erased and their place taken by others.	93
6.2.	**a** The early part of the classroom talk about the tug of war sought an explanation for the result of the competition. The different explanations (warrants) are contested, requiring data and warrants. **b** In the second part of the talk, the claim "we would have won" is discussed, and different warrants are produced—and themselves contested (rebutted).	97
6.3.	The setup of the tug of war using a separation of pulleys. There are two sets of pulleys. One set is attached to the railing (banister), whereas students pull on the other one. A third rope is attaché on one end to the banister, flows through the pulleys, and is pulled on by the teacher on the other end. The result is a five to one reduction of the student-supplied force.	99
7.1.	Although there is a continuous movement from finalizing the diagram(a) to laying down the chalk (b) to orienting in the direction of the opponent (c), and back to the diagram again, there are different in-order-tomotives in play, none of which can be explained in terms of a composite of bodyor mind.	111
7.2.	In normal situations where speakers are in agreement and aligned, the pitch levels of the next speaker tend to pick up where the preceding speaker has left off and then return to the second's speaker normal range. The non-aligned pitches manifest the same differences that also manifest themselves in other ways: the different positions that are worked out through scientific argumentation.	112

TABLES

3.1.	The claim-evidence covariation in reasoning.	43
3.2.	The joint space of classroom reasoning.	47
5.1.	Examples of children's claims and evidence on their science notebooks.	81

1

Argumentation Research in Science Education

Citizens in society are regularly confronted by diverse claims and decision-making actions with respect to health, food, energy saving plans, environmental security and so at personal, local, and global levels of life and wellbeing. Among diverse claims and action paths, it is it is imperative that citizens develop habits of mind to critically evaluate evidence and make decisions on such issues. One of the goals of science education is to enable students to become scientifically literate citizens who are equipped to engage in thoughtful deliberation about scientific discoveries and socioscientific issues through critical reasoning using scientific and social evidence. Contemporary curriculum in science is beginning to address this goal for scientific literacy by including real-life problems in the curriculum and by inviting students to consider competing claims and to search for relevant information regarding the issues.

Science educators and researchers have recognized that making informed decisions by coordinating evidence and knowledge claims is central to reasoning and problem solving in scientific discourse (Kuhn 1993; Mercer et al. 2004; Sampson and Clark 2008). Since argumentation is one form of interaction used by scientists to evaluate the credibility of claims and evidence, it has been recognized as an effective instructional strategy in school science to enhance students' scientific thinking and science culture (e.g. Driver et al. 2000; Duschl and Osborne 2002; Osborne et al. 2004). In the structure of argumentation, one is encouraged to provide and evaluate data and evidence to support or refute claims and to construct explanations that link between evidence and theories. Learning the interplay of claims, evidence, and justification in argumentation empowers students' confidence to use the languages of science and to develop criteria for knowledge evaluation and construction of scientific explanations (Jiménez-Aleixandre and Erduran 2007).

Argument in science classrooms can be distinguished from explanation based on the purpose, directionality, and uncertainty of knowledge claims (e.g. Osborne and Patterson 2011). Whereas scientific explanation is to explain and make sense of phenomena based on other scientific ideas or facts, argument is to justify a claim with evidence or persuade others that some claim is valid. In explanation, there is no doubt that the phenomena or notions to be explained are valid and accepted; but in argument, the claim could be confronted with counter claim and there thus exists uncertainty. The goal of argument is to diminish the uncertainty that goes with some claim by means of strongly justified warrants and backing so that the claim has a higher likelihood to get accepted. In argument, there is also a sense of directionality that goes from the premises to tentative conclusion through the process of developing warrant, backing, and rebuttal. In explanation, there already is a well-established fact that is later supported by less-than-certain explanation. Because argument is developed to reach justified, well-accepted conclusions, i.e. explanation, explanation and argument are complementarily connected and practiced (McNeill 2011). However, as the nature of argument requires the explicit performance of evaluating and justifying claims and evidence, it is recognized as an effective means for developing evidence-based reasoning skills in science classrooms.

Argument and argumentation are also used interchangeably in many studies of students' argumentation in science education. In the studies of students' argumentation skills, the logical structures of claim, evidence, and conclusion in students' talk and written texts are emphasized and examined to understand students' argumentation abilities. To consider the function of argumentation is to justify claims through evidence and good argumentation comes with good arguments, it is reasonable to study patterns and structures of arguments to understand students' argumentation skills. Yet, some researchers raise concerns that whereas the style of argument might be good the argumentation still could be weak (Biro and Siegel 2011). In this statement, argument and argumentation are different and share different criteria to evaluate its quality. The style is the form or pattern of augmentative talk and writing, that is, argument. Argumentation is the epistemic function that makes one's claim logical and convincing because of evidence. Distinction between argument as a product and argumentation as a process of argument is fundamental in terms of setting up pedagogical goals and implications (Andrews 2010). Arguments are structured sets of propositions to provide support for beliefs or assertions with justification which do not have room for dialectal or rhetorical considerations for speakers or writers, whereas argumentation involves the process of reasoning and arguing with different arguments, skills, and values in commutative interactions. In the argumentation process, arguers must process the contributions to communication others make, and thereby must anticipate and practice the cognitive burden to prove their own assertions (Kuhn 2010). In many existing studies, the terms argument and argumentation are often used interchangeably with the emphasis of the coherence between claim and evidence and justification in students' talk and writing as core value of argumentation.

Toulmin Argument Patterns

Many argumentation studies are based on the Toulmin Argument Pattern (TAP) (Toulmin 1958/2003), which has been the predominant paradigm for studying argumentation in science classrooms and science education research (e.g. Erduran et al. 2004; Roberts and Gott 2010; Simon 2008). Toulmin explained that arguments are field independent and the standards of arguments are valid for arguments in any field. The TAP model proposes evaluating the standards of arguments by means of major components of arguments: data, claims, warrants, backing for warrants, rebuttals, and modal qualifiers. The data (grounds) might consist of some facts or observed phenomena that are the base for a claim development (statement, conclusion, or assertion). A warrant is a component that links claim and data. In a warrant, there is a logical process of thinking and explaining why the data support the claim. Backing is to give additional support to the warrant to be true. Qualifiers or modal qualifiers are statements that put some conditions to make the claim true, for instance, under circumstances, the claim is true; otherwise it would not be. Examples of qualifiers are "unless," "usually," "probably," "possibly," and so forth. Rebuttals are discrepancies or exceptions to the claim. The structure of the argument, as Toulmin presented it in *The Uses of Argument,* features in Fig. 1.1, so that a typical argument might run like this:

> Data: Harry was born in Bermuda.
> Warrant: Since a man born in Bermuda will generally be a British subject
> Backing: on account of the following status and other legal provisions:
> Qualifier: So, presumably,
> Claim: Harry is a British subject
> Rebuttal: Unless both his parents were aliens, or he has become a naturalized American, or…

The TAP approach emphasizes the importance of warrant to logically link and evaluate the relationship between data and claim (Fig. 1.1). Backing supports the value of warrant to be true and rebuttals to make sure exceptions and discrepancies such as counterclaims are tested and refuted to reach a conclusion (confirming or changing the claim).

Science education researchers have adapted TAP to understand and develop features, categories and process of argumentation in science education. The modifications focus on the elements of claim and counter claim, evidence, and justification (warrants, backing, qualifiers) in students' argumentation. Some researchers regard the elements of claim, rebuttal, and justification as the most critical features of argumentation. When analyzing classroom data, they code those elements to examine the quantity and quality of students' argumentation in classrooms (e.g. Osborne et al. 2004). In the analytical framework of TAP, students' hypotheses, theories, and predictions, are coded as "claim" and data, grounds, backings, and qualifiers are often clustered as "evidence." Students' explanation to connect claim and evidence is categorized as "warrant" (justification). Taking into consideration

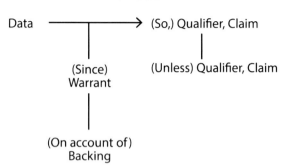

Fig. 1.1 The structure of an argument according to Toulmin (1958/2003)

opposite positions and ideas was taken another essential element of argumentation as "rebuttal," thus counted as a higher level of argumentation skill. Based on the presence and frequencies of these elements (claims, data, backing, warrants, rebuttals), an analytical framework was developed to examine students' argumentation from level 1 to 5. Similarly, the quality of argumentation was evaluated based on coding rubrics for the articulation of warrant, evidence for claims, and rhetorical references to data in student writing (Sandoval and Millwood 2005). To give a priory to conceptual quality in students' argumentation, these authors also focused on the articulation of science explanation, warrant of claims and data-driven claims, going beyond the normative standard approach of TAP. In the Science Writing Heuristic (SWH) approach, researchers used TAP components to understand how functions of language and argument components are developed and related in students' generative talk (generating arguments) and representational talk (represent their arguments in writing) (e.g. Cavagnetto et al. 2010). Here, TAP was adapted for analyzing students' arguments in relation to the functions of language (informative, interactional, heuristic, personal, instrumental, regulatory, and imaginative). The majority of students' arguments were claims and evidence and their arguments were evidently related to informative and heuristic functions of language. In other studies, the TAP approach was applied in combination with other theoretical frameworks or analytical tools. For instance, one study combined TAP approach with Lakatos' Programme Development to examine students' argumentation on socio-scientific issues (Chang and Chu 2008), whereas other studies combined TAP analytic framework with technological mapping tools to map out students' claim making and justification to examine the ability and process of students' argumentation (e.g. Okada and Shum 2008; Simon 2008). The TAP approach was also adapted to develop students' scientific literacy through school practical work (Gott and Duggan 2007). In practical work, students learn to make a public claim through analyzing a set of data, comparing with other sources of data, and evaluating their claims with wider issues such as counterclaims, bias, economy, and sociopolitical issues in social dimensions.

As the TAP-related literature in education research and practice expanded, investigators recognized that microstructural approach of the model might not be common practice in everyday and classroom talk and have extensively discussed the difficulties and limitation of TAP approach to the analysis of classroom talk (e.g. Duschl 2007; Kelly and Takao 2002; Nielsen, 2013). The categories that appear in TAP are interpreted inconsistently in data analysis (e.g. Osborne et al. 2004). With the ambiguity and inconsistency of TAP coding schemes, understanding the levels of argumentation is unclear and limited (e.g. Nussbaum 2011; van Eemeren et al. 1996). The TAP model primarily is a normative structural format of reasoning process, different from how people argue in many everyday communicative situations. It is difficult to analyze why and how students arrive at conclusions and how argumentation develops students' reasoning skills and knowledge, that is, epistemic criteria in students' argumentation process. Moreover, there is an assumption that students need to understand the various components of TAP argument in a logical fashion to demonstrate higher-level reasoning skills in their talk and writing. For instance, when students' argumentation skills are analyzed by means of TAP-based analytical tools, warrant, backing, and rebuttal (counter claims) have to be explicit in students' talk or texts to be coded as constituting a higher level of argument. This approach requires high levels of understanding argumentation structures and communication skills, and thus this could be more appropriate for students in higher grades with more sophisticated language skills and registers, thus not easily manageable to students without the proper language abilities (Naylor et al. 2007). Indeed, writing arguments in science classrooms requires certain levels of knowledge specific to science and language skills of lexicon and grammar to perform high levels of argumentation (Sandoval and Millwood 2005). In this approach, argumentation often is examined and learned through mastering arguments. This may explain why there is not much research on argumentation in the lower grades of elementary science classrooms.

Understanding argumentation as social dialogical process adds another layer of challenge to the TAP approach. In classroom situations, argumentation often emerges when students encounter different ideas and opinions during problem solving situations. When students attempt to reach conclusions or solutions to problems, they choose the best answers (claims, conclusions, solutions, etc.) by evaluating and justifying ideas (evidence). In classroom discussion, different members often state claim and evidence and warrant-making (linking claims and evidence) more often is done at a collective rather than individual level. In the process of argumentation, some warrants are implicit or unspoken when claims are accepted based on the suggested evidence. When claims are developed based on their collective knowledge built from previous classes then rebuttals do not seem necessary. The interlocutors' epistemic beliefs and premises are often implicitly embedded in dialogical argumentation, and these hidden backgrounds and premises cannot be explored by simply coding argument elements (Macagno and Konstantinidou 2013). Thus, examining the level of argumentation by coding elements is challenged within the dynamics of dialogical reasoning in classroom situations. Argumentation indeed can be analyzed by attending to argumentation sequences and argumentation cores and the dialectic features of dialogical argumentation can be understood by paying attention to sequential moves of reasoning, not by extrapolated core (TAP-based) elements (Nielsen 2013). Analysis by means of the TAP framework is appropriate to understand the cores of students' argumentation (i.e. arguments) but not sequences of reasoning, especially when students attempt to solve problems through classroom dialogues.

Dialogue and Presumptive Argumentation

In decision-making processes on complex issues in everyday lives, people tend to engage in argumentation discourse where ideas and claims are conflicting and complexly intertwined. There are a variety of competing claims and evidence with various levels of uncertainty in argumentation about those issues. In classroom practice, the uncertainty of those issues is sometimes scaled down when specific procedures are provided and alternatives are strictly limited for the purpose of helping students to arrive at conclusions that are already embedded in the task from the beginning of problem solving. In contrast, authentic argumentation on socioscientific issues involves multiple goals and often multiple agents, typically resulting in diverse set of possible solutions and alternatives. The fundamental nature of a socioscientific issue is that it is open to multiple views and dimensions of knowledge and skills so that arriving at a resolution out of this diversity is inevitably unpredictable with a certain level of uncertainty (Halverson et al. 2009). When students are engaged in a genuine problem solving process, they bring diverse ideas about the topic and their decision-making and conclusions emerge from the dynamic relationships of goals, agents involved and contexts. They learn how to make decisions with a certain level of uncertainty and complexity of problems. As a result, argumentation also becomes more dialogical. Such dialogical argumentation situated in social contexts is characteristic of everyday civic actions toward socioscientific and environmental problems. It is appropriate for developing students' science literacy.

There has been an approach to understanding students' argumentation by looking into the dynamics of interactive nature of argumentation and presumptive reasoning (Walton 1996). Unlike classical syllogistic forms of reasoning, which logically leads to a resolution, presumptive argumentation involves practical reasoning with many potential outcomes. Walton's argumentation schemes serve to illuminate the diversity of knowledge sources and epistemic beliefs students use to make arguments and the influences that contribute to how they evaluate competing arguments when forming a conclusion. This makes it possible to study the dynamic processes of argumentation in a dialogical setting, that is, how students evaluate each other's claims and evidence by raising critical questions and the way they collaboratively reach solutions. In this way, Walton's framework of presumptive argumentation is of value to account for students' epistemic engagements, reasoning sequences and types, and use of multiple evidence sources in their group discussions. These features are revealed through argumentation schemes and critical questions.

In Walton's framework, the whole discourse and patterns of an argumentative dialogue is understood in terms of an interplay of complex relations between argumentation schemes and critical questions. Argumentation schemes are patterns of making inferences in a dialogue (Walton 2006; Walton et al. 2008). Arguers use various types of reasons, knowledge, and evidence to express their position on a topic. Walton initially identified 26 argumentation schemes such as arguments from sign, arguments from position to know and expert opinions, arguments from analogy, arguments from commitment, arguments from popular opinion, and so forth. He provided a set of critical questions for each scheme and later developed more schemes with specific aspects of knowledge claim. Here is an example of a set of argument scheme and critical question for expert opinion.

Argument from expert opinion:

Dr W. Panzer, organic food tends to be free of added chemicals that many be harmful to your health. You should eat locally sourced, organic food.

Critical questions:

Expertise Questions: How credible (knowledgeable) is Dr Panzer as an expert source?

Field question: Is Dr Panzer an expert in the field?

Opinion question: What has Dr Panzer asserted that implies that argument?

Trustworthiness question: Is Dr Panzer personally reliable as a sourse, for example, is Dr Panzer biased?

Consistency question: Is the argument consistent with what other experts assert?

Backup evidence question: Is Dr Panzer's assertion based on evidence?

(Walton et al. 2008, p. 33)

Argumentation schemes are a way of identifying how and what one uses to argue, that is, the resources for knowledge claims. For example, when someone argues that using synthetic fertilizers is (not) an effective way to increase the size of the harvest in the long run, she can use scientist's explanation (expert opinion) or share her own experiences of growing vegetables in her garden (personal knowledge) or both. These schemes support tentative yet plausible arguments that need to be tested by critical questions which test the bases of argumentation schemes such as the implicit premises, background knowledge, and evidence that are being used (Macagno and Konstantinidou 2013). As seen in the preceding example, when making an argument from expert opinion, critical questions such as how credible the expert source is or whether the expert's assertion is based on evidence will strengthen the quality of argumentation. The proponents and respondents can employ argumentation schemes to promote the credibility of their position and use critical questions to reveal the viability of other positions and hidden premises. This is the process of practicing cognitive burden (Kuhn 2010) or shifting burden of proof (Walton 1988).

Depending on the purpose and dynamics of argumentative dialogues among the members of problem solving, types of argumentation could be identified as persuasion, negotiation, inquiry, information seeking, deliberation or eristic (Walton 2006). Persuasion dialogue starts with conflict of opinions and participants try to persuade other parties to change position and in that way to resolve the issue of conflict. Negotiation is a type of exchange that is used to reach partial agreements to settle conflicts and disagreements rather than persuading other parties to change their minds or taking one position over the other necessarily. Inquiry dialogue emerges when students attempt to find and verify evidence to prove or disprove suggested actions and hypothesis. Students collectively investigate certain issues and engage in problem solving without asking other parties to provide information or solutions. Information seeking is when one party presumably has information that the other party needs, and thus encourages the sharing of information. Deliberation is engaged to decide the best available course of action and to coordinate goals and actions in response to the perceived dilemma or practical choice. *Eristic* dialogue is dispute based on deeper and more personal conflict and bias. This type is not an ideal situation in argumentative dialogues, but happens in real-life situations. It requires teachers' attention and tactful support. The recognition of the types of argumentation dialogue reinforces argumentation needs to be understood as social action. In any type of argumentation, it is suggested that students practice critical questions toward argumentation schemes to demonstrate the quality of argumentation.

This approach of presumptive argumentation is particularly applicable to understand what sources of evidence students value and accept in their decision making on complex issues with multiple solutions and evidence sources available. Among various sources of knowledge and evidence, how do students evaluate and accept certain sources and evidence as plausible and trustworthy? What kind of critical questions are raised and how do they defend or give up their sources of knowledge and evidence? These questions are critical to understand students' epistemic criteria when engaged in argumentation dialogues.

Scientific Reasoning through Argumentation

Studies of argumentation in science classrooms discuss the importance of developing students' reasoning through argumentation in problem solving. When students are confronted with tasks, they are encouraged to justify their answers with evidence (e.g. science knowledge, experimental data). In the process of evaluating and justifying their thoughts and interpretations, they are to demonstrate the covariation between evidence (data) and conclusion (claim)—which is one of the core elements of scientific reasoning (Kuhn 1989). Claims are tested and justified through evaluating evidence and counter claims to strengthen the connection between the claim and evidence. Is this particular process necessary to good argumentation? What counts as good argumentation for classroom problem solving? Scholars have discussed certain categories of epistemic criteria to evaluate the quality of argumentation. They include the quality of knowledge and evidence, the coordination of claim and evidence, a complete set of data, examination of alternative and different ideas, and investigating the credibility of ways of evidence gathering (e.g. Ryu and Sandoval 2011; Sampson and Clark 2006). To understand the causal relationship between claim and evidence in students' arguments, researchers examine the presence of covariation between claim and evidence in students' explanation in controlled experimental designs (e.g. Kuhn 2011; Kuhn and Pearsall 2000) and students' writing on specific questions such as "what would happen if/when ..." (Ryu and Sandoval 2011). The presence of warrants and rebuttals were given priority in examining students' abilities of linking claim and evidence and evaluating alternative ideas against their claims as the quality of argumentation. In some research, the quality of evidence was particularly examined by looking into the appropriateness and sufficiency of scientific principles in claim-evidence-reasoning structure in students' argumentation texts (e.g. McNeill 2011). By acknowledging the limitations of TAP to understanding what and how students choose to monitor and evaluate arguments, researchers suggested to investigate how students choose the sources of evidence and practice justification through critical questions (e.g. Kim and Roth 2018). What counts as good argument and argumentation includes the dynamic democratic process of reasoning and evaluating ideas with ethical ethos among the members of problem-solving community (Erduran and Kaya 2016). Based on the diverse research on understanding the quality of student argumentation, it is evident that researchers tend to agree that students' reasoning and justifying with evidence for their knowledge claim is a critical aspect of argumentation.

Some pedagogical questions arise in terms of the practice of epistemic criteria in argumentation in classrooms. When argumentation is seen and taught as individual and structural arguments, rather than social and dialogical argumentation, epistemic criteria—e.g. such as the importance of testing evidence against alternatives—can be taught and practiced through step-by-step argument writing techniques. When argumentation is taught in this way, it is questionable how epistemic criteria be shared and practiced when the members of the communities are involved in argumentation in real time. When there are interruptions in students' reasoning process from other members in turn taking or interventions of classroom materials and curriculum focus, how would their reasoning and argumentation be affected? If argumentation is considered to be the structure of argument (e.g. TAP) or sets of argumentation schemes with critical questions (e.g. Walton's framework), teachers could explain what they are and how they can be practiced in one's reasoning and writing. Yet how those structures and elements of argumentation could be practiced when students are confronted with different and new ideas in classroom dialogues deserves further pedagogical attention. That is, it is questionable how someone who can demonstrate a quality of claim and evidence in writing will participate in argumentation dialogues when confronted by unexpected ideas and interactions. How would one value and practice the epistemic criteria to resolve the conflicts? Considering learning as the non-linear development of social action, teaching and learning argumentation also needs to be approached in the context of social interactions. When learning is considered as interpersonal process that precedes the individual deployment of a social practice (Vygotsky 1978), the meaning, function, and epistemic criteria of argumentation also need to be experienced and practiced in social relation first for further development.

In this regard, we explore in this book how argumentation emerges and is experienced as/in/through social actions and how the quality of argumentation as part of scientific reasoning could be shared and experienced among children, teacher, curriculum and classroom materials in elementary classrooms. The overview of this book is as follows.

Overview

This book is designed to present research about the teaching and learning of argumentation in elementary school science classroom. The book thereby prepares new ground, for the teaching and research of argumentation tends to be more typical in secondary school science. In part this is so because teaching approaches favor the equivalent of teaching grammar before teaching a language, whereas younger children may benefit from engaging in interesting and contested issues as a basis for developing an understanding of the structures that such debates take. All the while taking existing research as the starting point for our presentation, we also develop new approaches. These draw on a framework developed based on ideas that Vygotsky was beginning to articulate just prior to his untimely death. In the following, we outline the content of the chapters that follow.

The improvement of science education following the Sputnik shock was associated with an increasing formalization of theories and methods science educators used. Initially, the theories were highly individualistic based on J. Piaget's constructivism and the emergent psychological paradigm of information processing. In the late 1980s, science educators began to turn toward constructivism, an epistemology worked out to considerable extent by the Kantian philosopher E. von Glasersfeld. During the last decade of the 20th century, however, there has been an increasing focus on the role of the social in learning. The theories of the cultural-historical psychologist L. S. Vygotsky became one of the key influences on education general. However, given the poor translations of his work from Russian into English, it is not surprising that the real nature of his work is largely misrepresented. Even more importantly, most scholars have not realized that by the end of his life, Vygotsky has become very critical of his own work as too intellectualist and Cartesian. He completely rejected his earlier work, beginning to develop a new perspective. This new perspective has three aspects in particular that are important to science learning: (a) body and mind are manifestations of one and the same substance; (b) any higher psychological function *was* a social relation first; and (c) personality is the ensemble of societal relations. In chapter 2 ("Vygotsky's Spinozist Perspectives on Language"), we articulate the later Vygotsky's theory in view of developing a theoretical framework for understanding how children know and learn through argumentation in science classrooms.

Children's reasoning in problem solving is the topic of chapter 3. Educators have come to recognize children's critical thinking and problem solving skills as crucial contexts for the development of scientific literacy. There has been a widespread emphasis on argumentation as a way of developing critical and creative minds. Recent studies of children's reasoning have suggested that problem solving contexts contextualize and develop learners' thinking and learning within shared frameworks of knowledge as learners collectively talk, signify, and justify their interpretation of observed phenomena. With the dynamics of diverse knowledge and communication, argumentative discourse emerges and further develops children's intellectual capabilities to think and talk. When children participate in collective problem solving, often with the teacher, a joint intellectual realm of learning emerges to co-construct new thinking, reasoning, and thus learning. The notion of thinking and reasoning as social action becomes salient. In this chapter, we share classroom examples to discuss how reasoning and argumentation emerge and develop as collectives and how the importance of evidence is recognized when children and teacher participate together in classroom-based problem solving.

In chapter 4 entitled "Argumentation as Social Action," we exemplify and explain how children's argumentation emerges and develops through/as social action through empirical classroom data. Argumentation clearly is a higher psychological function. In regards to all higher psychological functions, societal-historical psychologists emphasize that these *are* societal relations before they are observed in the actions of individuals. To exemplify the emergence of higher function, consider the case of pointing. First, a child moves his hand arm or perhaps attempts to grasp an object; then the mother *treats* the movement *as* a gesture by taking the object in the extension of the arm and by reaching it to the child; and finally the child begins to point. Here, the higher function—intentional pointing—*was* a mother–child relation first. The fact that this occurred *in* a social relation is a case for the social nature of pointing, because it makes it possible that infants learn to point on their own. We provide empirical evidence of children's argumentation emerging and developing through classroom interactions to discuss argumentation as social relation between people first before it is an attribute that can be attached to an individual student.

Most scholars claiming adherence to the Vygotsky school of thought use the concept of *mediation* to explain the function of physical objects in human relation. In "the Role of Physical Objects in Science Lessons" (chapter 5), we problematize the concept and the approaches that draw on the concept. There is some legitimation in the writings of the earlier Vygotsky, who considered objects (artifacts, tools, signs) to stand *between* two people or *between* a person and her brain. Only during the last year of his life, Vygotsky moved away from this position on mediation recognizing—following the German philosopher L. Feuerbach—that an object, to play any role in their (verbal) exchanges, has to be a reality for two people.

Objects are important in science education, which is why there has been so much emphasis on "hands-on" activities. Currently there is no research on argumentation concerned with the function of objects in students' argumentation. In this chapter, we develop a late-Vygotskian perspective on the role of objects and tools in argumentation. We exhibit the constitutive relation between argumentation and objects because the former brings the latter into the accented visible. That is, one function of the argumentative talk is the augmentation and change in the accented visible that is the focus of the argumentative talk.

In the social studies of science, the notion of *inscription* replaces what psychologists call external representation. Inscriptions include diagrams, mathematical equations, tables, figures, and everything else other than text that is used in the sciences to stand for natural phenomena. Inscriptions not only appear in scientific journal articles and science textbooks but also, and perhaps more importantly, are integral features in face-to-face debates, where they have a number of additional functions—e.g. conscription (bringing people together), tool for social thinking, and boundary object. In chapter 6 ("Argumentation Over and About Inscriptions"), we exhibit the function of inscriptions in the argumentation of elementary students. As part of the debate about why a group of students lost a tug of war against their teacher, the chalkboard comes to be filled with student (and teacher) diagrams of real and hypothetical setups of the tug of war. The chapter analyzes and explains the function of these drawings in children's argumentation.

During the last decade of the 20th century, theoretical developments in the social sciences also included an increasing attention to discourse. The intellectualization of human behavior observable in the constructivist attention to mental structures was reborn in theories of discourse. As a result, everything related to scientific knowledge was said to exist as discourse and to be social construction. Cartesianism was simply reincarnated in new form. In chapter 7 ("Argumentation and the Thinking Body"), we develop a late-Vygotskian view on argumentation that goes beyond the body–mind dichotomy clearly apparent in other current approaches (among others, in the intellectualist orientations that these take). Taking the lead from the Russian philosopher E. V. Il'enkov—who had articulated a philosophical basis for the later Vygotsky's Spinozist approach that recognized the unity/identity of body and mind—we unfold a theoretical approach to understanding the development of children's argumentation practices that overcomes the body–mind dichotomy. The resultant theoretical position erases the distinction between knowing a language (i.e. the genre of argumentation) and knowing one's way around the world more generally consistent with Vygotsky's realization that the *sense* of a word depends on one's practical understanding of how the world works; in other words, the sense of a word depends on knowing one's way around the world.

In chapter 8 ("Teaching for Argumentation in Elementary Science"), we discuss how argumentation could be implemented in elementary science classrooms for children's reasoning and problem solving. Collaborative problem solving contexts provide rich learning experiences of reasoning, talking, negotiating and justifying ideas and further develop the emergence of argumentation as embodied and social action. As teachers play a significant role in engaging students in a high level of reasoning and argumentation, teachers' awareness and pedagogical strategies for the implementation of argumentation are critical. In this chapter, based on the late-Vygotskian view we articulate and exemplify throughout this book, we suggest teaching strategies of argumentation through problem solving contexts for classroom implementation.

References

Andrews, R. (2010). *Argumentation in higher education: Improving practice through theory and research*. New York, NY: Routledge.

Biro, J., & Siegel, H. (2011). Argumentation, arguing, and arguments: Comments on giving reasons. *Theoria, 26*(3), 279–287.

Cavagnetto, A., Hand, B. M., & Norton-Meier, L. (2010). The nature of elementary student science discourse in the context of the science writing heuristic approach. *International Journal of Science Education, 32*(4), 427–449.

Chang, S., & Chiu, M. (2008). Lakatos' scientific research programmes as a framework for analysing informal argumentation about socio-scientific issues. *International Journal of Science Education, 30*(13), 1753–1773.

Driver, R., Newton, P., & Osborne, J. F. (2000). Establishing the norms of scientific argumentation in classrooms. *Science Education, 84*(2), 287–312.

Duschl, R. (2007). Quality argumentation and epistemic criteria. In S. Erduran & M. P. Jimenez-Aleixandre (Eds.), *Argumentation in science education* (pp. 159–175). Dordrecht: Springer.

Duschl, R., & Osborne, J. F. (2002). Supporting and promoting argumentation discourse in science education. *Studies in Science Education, 38*(1), 39–72.

Erduran, S., & Kaya, E. (2016). Scientific argumentation and deliberative democracy: An incompatible mix in school science? *Theory into Practice, 55*(4), 302–310.

Erduran, S., Simon, S., & Osborne, J. F. (2004) TAPing into argumentation: Developments in the application of Toulmin's argument pattern for studying science discourse. *Science Education, 88*(6), 915–933.

Gott, R., & Duggan, S. (2007). A framework for practical work in science and scientific literacy through argumentation. *Research in Science & Technological Education, 25*(3), 271–291.

Halverson, K., Siegel, M., & Freyermuth, S. (2009): Lenses for framing decisions: Undergraduates' decision making about stem cell research. *International Journal of Science Education, 31*(9), 1249–1268.

Jimenez-Aleixandre, M. P., & Erduran, S. (2007). Argumentation in science education: An overview. In S. Erduran & M. P. Jimenez-Aleixandre (Eds.), *Argumentation in science education* (pp. 3–27). Dordrecht: Springer.

Kelly, G. J., & Takao, A. (2002). Epistemic levels in argument: An analysis of university oceanography students' use of evidence in writing. *Science Education, 86*, 314–342.

Kim, M., & Roth, W.-M. (2018). Dialogical argumentation in elementary science classrooms. *Cultural Studies of Science Education*, 1–25. doi:10.1007/s11422-017-9846-9

Kuhn, D. (1989). Children and adults as intuitive scientists. *Psychological Review, 96*(4), 674–689.

Kuhn, D. (1993). Science as argument: Implications for teaching and learning scientific thinking. *Science Education, 77*(3), 319–337.

Kuhn, D. (2010). Teaching and learning science as argument. *Science Education, 94*(5), 810–824.

Kuhn, D. (2011). What is scientific thinking and how does it develop? In U. Goswami (Ed.), *Handbook of childhood cognitive development* (pp. 497–523). Chichester: Blackwell.

Kuhn, D., & Pearsall, S. (2000). Developmental origins of scientific thinking. *Journal of Cognition and Development, 1*, 113–129.

Macagno, F., & Konstantinidou, A. (2013). What students' arguments can tell us: Using argumentation schemes in science education. *Argumentation, 27*(3), 225–243.

McNeill, K. L. (2011). Elementary students' views of explanation, argumentation and evidence and abilities to construct arguments over the school year. *Journal of Research in Science Teaching, 48*(7), 793–823.

Mercer, N., Dawes, L., Wegerif, R., & Sams, C. (2004). Reasoning as a scientist: Ways of helping children to use language to learn science. *British Educational Research Journal, 30*(3), 359–377.

Naylor, S., Keogh, B., & Downing, B. (2007). Argumentation and primary science. *Research in Science Education, 37*(1), 17–39.

Nielsen, J. A. (2013). Dialectical features of students' argumentation: A critical review of argumentation studies in science education. *Research in Science Education, 43*, 371–393.

Nussbaum, E. M. (2011). Argumentation, dialogue theory, and probability modeling: Alternative frameworks for argumentation research in education. *Educational Psychologist, 46*(2), 84–106.

Okada, A., & Shum, S. B. (2008). Evidence-based dialogue maps as a research tool to investigate the quality of school pupils' scientific argumentation. *International Journal of Research and Method in Education, 31*(3), 291–315.

Osborne, J. F., Erduran, S., & Simon, S. (2004). Enhancing the quality of argumentation in school science. *Journal of Research in Science Teaching, 41*(10), 994–1020.

Osborne, J. F., & Patterson, A. (2011). Scientific argument and explanation: A necessary distinction? *Science Education, 95*(4), 627–638.

Roberts, D., & Gott, S. (2010). Questioning the evidence for a claim in a socio-scientific issue: An aspect of scientific literacy. *Research in Science & Technological Education, 28*(3), 203–226.

Ryu, S., & Sandoval, W. (2012). Improvements to elementary children's epistemic understanding from sustained argumentation. *Science Education, 96*(3), 488–526.

Sampson, V., & Clark, D. B. (2008). Assessment of the ways students generate arguments in science education: Current perspectives and recommendations for future directions. *Science Education, 92*(3), 447–472.

Sandoval, W. A., & Millwood, K. (2005). The quality of students' use of evidence in written scientific explanations. *Cognition and Instruction, 23*(1), 23–55.

Simon, S. (2008). Using Toulmin's argument pattern in the evaluation of argumentation in school science. *International Journal of Research and Method in Education, 31*(3), 277–289.

Toulmin, S. (1958/2003). *The uses of argument.* Cambridge: Cambridge University Press.

van Eemeren, F. H., Grootendorst, R., Henkemans, F. S., Blair, J. A., Johnson, R. A., Krabbe, E. C. W., & Zarefsky, D. (1996). *Fundamentals of argumentation theory.* Mahwah, NJ: Lawrence Erlbaum Associates.

Vygotsky, L. S. (1978). *Mind in society: The development of higher psychological processes.* Cambridge, MA: Harvard University Press.

Walton, D. (1988). Burden of proof. *Argumentation, 2*, 233–254.

Walton, D. (1996). *Argumentation schemes for presumptive reasoning.* Mahwah, NJ: Lawrence Erlbaum Associates.

Walton, D. (2006). *Fundamentals of critical argumentation.* New York, NY: Cambridge University Press.

Walton, D., Reed, C., & Macagno, F. (2008). *Argumentation schemes.* New York, NY: Cambridge University Press.

2

Vygotsky's Spinozist Perspectives on Language

One psychologist more than any other has influenced theories of learning and development: Lev S. Vygotsky, sometimes referred to as the Mozart of psychology. It turns out, however, that he is known and celebrated for theory that he all but abandoned near the end of his life. Some recent publications suggest that much of the way in which Vygotsky's work has been taken up does injustice to what the psychologist had actually been writing to the point of totally misrepresenting the work. In the early years of this 21st century, Vygotsky's relatives provided E. Iu. Zavershneva with access to the family archive. This researcher discovered a wealth of previously unseen personal notes. In those notes that were written during the last two years of his life, Vygotsky expresses discontent with his own preceding work and theory: precisely the one that most readers somehow are familiar with. Vygotsky was in the process of developing a complete overhaul and revision of his theoretical approach. The early effects of his revisions can be seen in the final texts that he wrote and that were posthumously published. This includes the first and the last chapter of *Thinking and Speech* (Vygotsky 1987) and the analysis of the historical *The Teaching about Emotion* (Vygotsky 1999). The latter text was to be the introductory part to his unfinished *A Theory of Emotion*. In a note pertaining to the dedication of the book, the text reads: "The book of my whole life, is poorly written, but its thoughts are mine.—What becomes outdated is what relates to the evils of the day" (Vygotsky in Zavershneva 2010a, p. 40). This note reflects the fact that although Vygotsky had spent much of his scholarly life critiquing the Cartesian dualism then as much as now characteristic of psychology, he failed to overcome it in his earlier work. He did recognize remnants of Cartesian dualism in his work, including an over-emphasis of the intellectual over affect and the practical. The turn to the writings of the Dutch philosopher B. Spinoza, which he read through the Marxian lens of *The German Ideology* (Marx and Engels 1978). The later book had been published for the first time during the final 18 months of his life. In 1932, the Central Committee of the Soviet Socialist Party published a German version; a Russian version followed in 1933, the year before Vygotsky died.

Even though Vygotsky was foreshadowing a way to overcome the Cartesianism in psychology, the Cartesianism that he critiqued characterizes current theoretical approaches, especially constructivism. To overcome Cartesianism, Vygotsky was turning to Spinoza. Philosophers continue to debate whether Spinoza really overcomes dualism. Here we follow those who develop a non-dualist theory based on Spinoza's writing, especially when read through a Marxian lens. Spinoza had postulated that there is only one substance. It has body (extension) and thought as two of its infinitely numbered attributes. That is, there were not two substances, a biological body and a cultural (societal) thought (mind)—sometimes conceptualized in the opposition of nature and nurture—but only one substance. That substance itself is invisible and inaccessible; but it manifests itself in different ways, with body and mind being the most relevant to understand human existence.[1] This one substance is the thinking body. This thinking body, however, is not the individual human body: "Thought can … only be understood through investigation of its mode of action in the system thinking body–nature as a whole" (Il'enkov 1977, p. 52). Spinoza importantly noted that there was no way to get from the attributes to the substance. That is, as soon as we begin thinking about and researching human practices from the perspective of the (biological) body, then we cannot get to thought (mind); and when we begin thinking about and researching human practices from the perspective of thought (mind), we cannot get to the (biological) body. This is the contradiction that Vygotsky points out in a number of his writings: Psychology was and continues to be stuck. But Vygotsky did not take on Spinoza wholesale. He realized that there were some problems in Spinoza's work. He felt that Spinoza should be read through a Marxian lens generally and through the lens of *The German Ideology* specifically.

Unfortunately, Vygotsky was able only to begin reworking of his theory. In the last personal note that he wrote prior to entering the hospital where he died only 30 days later on June 11, 1934, he likened himself to Moses: having seen the Promised Land, he was never allowed to enter it. What was it that Vygotsky had seen and that he wanted to develop for a social psychology to come? More importantly, how would we thinking about knowing and learning today if Vygotsky had actually been able to do what he envisioned? Might his inclination to the writings of Marx have deterred Western scholars to translate his works that first became available during the Cold War period? What would theories of reasoning and thinking in science education look like if we were to follow the lines of theorizing apparent from the notes of the late Vygotsky (i.e. during the last 18 months of his life)? The intent of this book is in part to show where such a revision takes us in science education generally and in the area of argumentation specifically. To write about, theorize, and research argumentation requires us to consider language and its relation to thinking.

---

[1] A similar idea exists in quantum mechanics, where the state of a quantum particle, described by its wave function, is not visible or known. In a measurement process, however, the quantum particle reveals this or that characteristic.

The Real Life of Language

There are presuppositions concerning the workings of language and our ways to work with language that do not bear out upon closer inspection. Among such presuppositions is that about communicating. It is generally assumed that one person speaks; the recipient then interprets what has been said and replies. However, this cannot be the real story of the life of language. This is so because in many conversations, the recipient immediately replies and sometimes begins to reply even before the first speaker has completed. Even if we take into account that teachers have been reported to wait about 0.8 seconds or that the standard maximum silence between two speakers is about 1 second, there would not be enough time to comprehend, interpret, and then begin a reply. Thus, cognitive scientists studying Tetris players showed that it would take about 1.5 seconds to mentally rotate one of the simple figures falling into the screen from its top margin. Then they would have to interpret the position with respect to the existing configuration on the bottom; and then they could act. If humans were indeed to play Tetris in this way, they would be far slower than they actually are. How much more complex is the comprehension of a phrase, followed by an interpretation to get at its "meaning," and then a construction of a reply? A related presupposition is that a word belongs to the speaker—in the way a scientific research article or a book is attributed to the author/s. While the saying is taking place, the recipient is treated as inactive, a mere recipient filled with the talk of the other. Because the meaning of a phrase is given by the phrase as a whole, the interpreter would not be able to begin an interpretation until after speaking has ended. In the transcription of research data, these latter presuppositions are embodied in the common ways in which transcriptions are represented. Consider Fragment 2.1, which comes from the talk of a mixed sixth- and seventh-grade class of an elementary school in Western Canada. Aslam and his group members have designed and constructed the prototype of a machine in response to call for proposals. They are currently presenting their design prototype to the class, the members of which raise questions and voice critique. In this particular instance, Leanne voices what—in a phrase that takes the form of a reply—is treated as a question (turn 1). It can be noticed that there is argumentative reasoning involved: a crank is not useful in this design *because* the winch has to go back and forth (horizontally), and thus there is no way that it could be brought into its initial state ("reloaded").

Fragment 2.1
  1 L: how come you didn't use a crank for moving it there?
  2 A: how could you put a crank here? because you can't just make it go one way because then you have to reload it again, it has to be going back and forth.
  3 L: oh, okay.

Readers familiar with the analysis of classroom conversation will immediately note that the exchange does not take the form of the often-reviled initiation-reply-

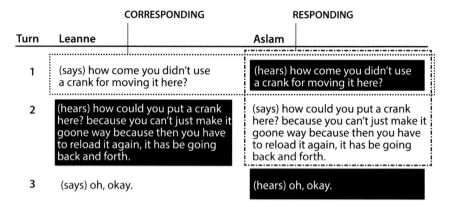

Fig. 2.1 This revised transcription of Fragment 2.1 includes the simultaneous actions of the recipients resulting in an inherently social *trans*action of *corresponding*. The reply arises in and from attending and receiving speech, which together constitute the phenomenon of *responding*. It, too, is a transaction and thus social through and through.

evaluation (IRE) form. Turn 3 constitutes an acknowledgment of the information provided in turn 2, and thus is not in the form of an evaluation. The common way in which such an exchange is approached assumes that Aslam interprets what Leanne has said and then respond. Moreover there is no pause between the ending of the first phrase and the beginning of the next. As stated above, Aslam could not have interpreted the preceding phrase until it has ended because its content can be established only when it is available as a whole. But Aslam did not stand there inactive while Leanne was speaking—in general, we are not inactive when we listen to another person. Instead we actively orient toward the speech and receive what is directed at us. That is, while the sound-words are arising from the vibrating vocal cords and other speech organs of the speaker, they are *simultaneously* ringing in the ears of the recipient. While a first person is saying something, the other is hearing it—if this is not the case, then we might have a second turn of this kind: "Did you say something to me? I didn't hear. Do you mind repeating?" or "What'd you say?" If we want to render the speech situation more completely, involving all actions, then we need to revise our transcription (Fig. 2.1).

The revised transcription shows that the word is in common to the speaker and recipient. This is the point that Vygotsky (1987) makes in the final paragraphs of *Thinking and Speech*, where he writes: "In consciousness the word is what—in Feuerbach's words—is absolutely impossible for one person but possible for two" (p. 285). He continues by noting that the word is a manifestation of human consciousness. Language goes with consciousness, and consciousness, as Marx and Engels (1978) point out, is as ancient as language. We observe here a shift from an instrumentalist view of language—language as a tool that somehow stands between two people who are opposed and impervious to each other like two monads—to a perspective where language not only is common to the communicators but also constitutive of their very relation. The word, language, or phrase—e.g.

"how come you didn't use a crank for moving it here" (turn 1)—*is* the relation between Leanne and Aslam. Without the speaking event, there is no relation in this particular situation. The phrase here manifests *con*sciousness, their knowing (Lat. *scire*) together (Lat. *co[m,n]-*). Not only do both know that the content of the phrase pertains to the absence of a crank in the prototype design but also they know that the phrase is to function as a question. They also know how to act in the preferred manner, which is to produce a phrase that functions as a reply.

A look at the revised transcription shows that each phrase in the *com*munication—something we have in common, share, with another—belongs to both participants. We thus have to change our thinking about what is happening. This is so because we no longer can say that the phrase "how come you didn't use a crank for moving it there?" is a single speech act, for Aslam is acting *at the same time*. Aslam is actively *attending to* and *receiving* what is coming even before knowing what exactly it is. Attending to and receiving are part of the "attitude toward the other's consciousness, part of an "internal polemic with another and with himself," leading to "an endless dialogue where one reply begets another, which begets a third, and so on" (Bakhtin 1984, p. 230). Thus, we indeed are dealing not with an interaction, where one action (speaking) is followed by another (replying), but with a *trans*action: *corresponding*. The transaction of corresponding includes the ensemble of speaking and actively attending/receiving. It therefore represents a coming and going, involving both participants. The transaction therefore cannot be reduced to any one individual. The transaction belongs to both; indeed, it constitutes the two individuals as the relevant speaker and recipient.

Some readers may raise the objection that the "meaning" of a phrase may be different for participants in a translocution—though there is no evidence in the present case, as the acknowledgment (turn 3) following the reply (turn 2) also manifests that the latter has satisfactorily completed the preceding query (turn 1). Of course, whatever the respective "meanings" may be—e.g. something in the head of each Aslam and Leanne—is irrelevant to the unfolding of the situation. Only what each participant makes available to the other is relevant to the next transaction. It therefore has been suggested that we think of the two parties (here Aslam and Leanne) "as two eyes, each giving a monocular view of what goes on and, together, giving a binocular view in depth. This double view *is* their relationship" (Bateson 1979, p. 133). Near the end of his life, Vygotsky (1987), who most of his scholarly career emphasized meaning in the head of the individual, notes in the spirit of his emerging Marxian-Spinozist take on language, "language is consciousness that exists in practice for other people and therefore for myself" (Vygotsky 1987, p. 285). In the same vein, though on the basis of very different philosophical commitments, it has been noted that "meaning" is an effect of the relation (Vološinov 1930), where a relation is an event inherently spread out in space and time. Signification (Rus. *znachenie*, "meaning") therefore "does not reside in the word or in the soul of the speaker or in the soul of the listener. Signification is the *effect of the interaction between speaker and listener on the material of a given sound complex*" (p. 104). All three scholars thus emphasize what is common between two speakers, language and consciousness, rather than what is different. Instead of focusing on possible differences in "meaning," all three point to the inherently shared nature of "meaning" and consciousness that manifests itself in the language used.

This approach has consequences for how we have to think about the participants in communication, for the relationship neither belongs nor is internal to any one individual. Some observers of the science lesson involving these two students talked about the aggressiveness that could be observed (e.g. could be heard in the particular intonations); and they also talked about the pride that individuals and groups exhibited. But words such as "aggressiveness" or "pride," which observers of the whole session involving Leanne and Aslam might ascribe as characteristics to the two students, respectively, "have their roots in what happens between persons, not in some something-or-other inside the person" (p. 133). Such terms therefore are characteristic of relations rather than individuals.

The revised transcription features a second type of transaction: *responding* (Fig. 2.1). While the words of the other are ringing in the ears of the recipient, he orients toward a reply, which begins to form simultaneously. The origin of the reply therefore is not the finished phrase but the speaking itself. Instead, the orientation toward and origin of the reply lies in the actively attending and receiving part. Moreover, the orienting toward the speech of the other is not finished with the speech but, because of the time it takes to grasp and interpret—if this actually happens in the way we commonly tend to think about these events—extends over the entire reply. The category *responding* covers both event forms: *actively attending to/receiving from* and *replying to*. The two cannot be understood independently, for the second event arises in and from the former. Indeed, it has been suggested that the understanding of a phrase relates to the subsequent turn "as one line of dialogue to the next" (Vološinov 1930, p. 104). That is, understanding is dialogical, existing in the relation between actively attending to/receiving from and replying to another person. Understanding therefore is transactional, literally consisting of two actions moving in different directions and, in communication, involving different individuals.

There is something else to be taken into account when considering transcriptions: the fact that speakers orient their speech to specific recipients. The phrase—its language, content, and even complexity and grammar—takes into account the recipient. Leanne is not speaking to her teachers present in the class; she is not talking to her parents about the things she has done in that day's science class; and she is not explaining to her kid sister what she has done in school. Instead, Leanne is addressing Aslam—not in the schoolyard but in the here-and-now of the science lesson in the presence of her classmates and the two teachers. The speech *takes into account* all of these contextual features generally and the intended recipient specifically. Not only does her phrase take into account the recipient and context—discussion and critique of a design prototype—but also it is shaped to solicit a particular kind of next turn on the part of the recipient. The (socially) preferred type of next turn comes with Aslam's "reply." Readers will be familiar with many standard turn pairs, including query–reply, invitation–acceptance, order–following, instruction–following, and affirmation–dis/agreement. The first parts have to be shaped grammatically and intonationally in particular ways to solicit intended reaction from the specific recipient. This is thus another way in which the phrase takes into account the other so that it cannot be singularly attributed to the speaker. We do know that events can and do turn out differently then intended. Thus, the present classroom event certainly would have taken a different turn and evolved in different ways had turn 2 consisted of something like, "Why do you have to be so aggressive?" or "Don't treat me like a little kid." Then another type of turn pair would have been produced, and those presents would now have had to deal with the noted aggression or the insult. But here there are not hidden "meanings" that are at stake. Instead, the second person makes visible aggressiveness or insult, and it is precisely because this is now part of consciousness of the situation, it will have to be addressed, where not directly addressing it will be a particular way of addressing the issue.

If a phrase does take all of this into account, then the phrase (language, content, and grammar) cannot be attributed to Leanne alone, it cannot be reduced to any properties that are particular to her singular being (individual mind). The language that she articulates has come to her from the other and therefore is not her own. Indeed, if a language were completely one's own, if there were something of that nature, then others could not understand it and it would not be language in the sense that we use this term. At this point, therefore, it no longer surprises to read what Vygotsky (1987) wrote near the end of his life: "The word absorbs intellectual and affective content from the *entire context* in which it is intertwined" (p. 276, emphasis added). Up to this point we considered only the intellectual aspects of speech. The quotation also suggests that the word absorbs the affective content from the context. How might this be?

We already note that a recipient may *feel* aggressed or insulted. Common constructivist approaches to such phenomena tend to treat what people feel as an effect of an interpretation. But when we attend to someone speaking, we do not know what is coming at us, passive as we are with respect to what is received. We may feel aggressed or insulted even before speaking has ended. Feeling does not mean having interpreted something. Feeling is an affect. The framework laid out here allows us to understand this affective dimension of speaking. Thus, when we attend to the speech of another, as Aslam certainly had to do to be able to reply, we also open up to receive. This makes us vulnerable. In fact, while receiving the words we orient toward the next turn, the replique, without knowing *what* we are receiving. We are affected by the speech of another without knowing the cause. Again, if constructivists were right, then our interpretation only depends on ourselves. Why would we go through the efforts of interpreting something as an insult given that we know it will hurt? Interpreting something as an insult means that we are hurting ourselves. Moreover, we would know about the causes of the insult: our own interpretation of words that do not constitute information coming in from the outside—as constructivists insist—but which is completely constructed on the inside.

Many scholars have pointed out that we do not have access to our *thinking* and only to our thoughts. These thoughts are available, for example, in articulated speech or in any other sign form that we may produce. Thus, "thought is not expressed but completed in the word" (Vygotsky 1987, p. 250). In a way, the speaking individual *is ahead of itself* in the sense that s/he speaks before s/he knows or can grasp what it will have said once speaking has ended. The Russian word Vygotsky used and translated as *thought* (i.e. mysl') may also be translated as *thinking*. In this case, therefore, it is thinking that is not expressed but completed in the word. Let us consider this statement in the context of the revised transcription (Fig. 2.1). Take the position of Aslam. We note above that the reply he articulates (turn 2) arises in and from the preceding turn. However, Aslam cannot know the effect that the said will have on Leanne. This he can find out only from the next action (turn 3). That is, the origin of turn 2 lies in turn 1, and its effect becomes available in turn 3. All of this acting is associated with activity in and of the brain even though we are not conscious of precisely what it is—we hear something as a question or insult without knowing why we hear it thus. But it is part of the event of thinking. Thus, thinking with respect to the phrase "how could you put a crank here? because you can't just make it go one way because then you have to reload it again, it has to be going back and forth" reaches from turn 1 to turn 3. It solves a specific function and fulfills a task. It unfolds, and thus has movement. Thinking, Vygotsky (1987) writes, establishes a connection between concrete things, which, in the present situation, is the original phrase getting thinking going in turn 1 and the effect of the words, available in turn 3. The task of the investigator resides in establishing "the relationship of thought and word as a movement," "as a transition from thought to word and from word to thought" (p. 250). We solve this task above in our analysis of the active attention and reception that leads into speaking, which is followed by the active attention and reception required to evaluate the effect that speaking has had.

In this section, we cover considerable and sufficient ground to understand how children learn to participate in argumentation and why they will eventually produce complete forms of argumentation in their own behavior. Detailed descriptions of these topics are found in subsequent chapters. Throughout this chapter and in this section specifically, we mark our distance from the notion of "meaning," especially the idea of meaning as being something specific to individuals, somehow lodged in their minds or thinking. Indeed, historians with access to Vygotsky's personal notes acknowledge that there was a shift near the end of his life from a singular focus on "meaning" toward a broader orientation to *sense* and *consciousness*. Thus, initially "the way to consciousness through *word meaning* was the only opportunity available to Vygotsky, despite its limitation" so that "intellectualistic bias dominated in all his empirical studies of the development of word meaning" (Zavershneva 2014, p. 78). He shifted toward the notions of *sense* and the *sense-giving field*; but he never was given the time to work out where such a shift might lead. If he had been aware of some scholarship that simultaneously occurred in the West, including phenomenology and phenomenological sociology, then he would have found part of a worked out approach (Schütz 1932). We turn to elaborating a shift from meaning, understood as that which the word signifies, to sense and the sense-giving field.

From Meaning to Sense

In the preceding section, we quote Vygotsky writing that thinking is not expressed but completed in the word. The word, therefore, does not signify something behind it, a thought, an idea, or a concept. This reading of Vygotsky's statement therefore explodes the traditional use of the term "meaning," which is taken in the sense of a signified that is made present in communication by means of the word, the signifier. During the last two years of his life, Vygotsky had come to the limit of the usefulness of his work on word meaning. It is only a small part of a bigger problem of sense. Thus, "meaning is only one of these zones of the sense that the word acquires in the context of speech" whereas "a word's sense is the aggregate of all psychological facts that arise in our consciousness as a result of the word. Sense is a dynamic, fluid, and complex formation which has several zones that vary in their stability" (Vygotsky 1987, p. 275–276). A number of specialists on the later Vygotsky's work suggest that the idea of language as a sense-giving field was a dominant theme in the thinking of the psychologist (e.g. El'konin 1994). Vygotsky never got to work out a theory of sense, detail what those zones might be, or make a suggestion how this field might be subdivided into (structured by) zones. However, already two years before his death, a relevant book was published in Vienna with the literally translated title of "The Sense-filled Structure of the Social World: An Introduction into Understanding-oriented Sociology" (Schütz 1932). We do not doubt that Vygotsky would have found that the book was in line with his own developing thinking. In it, the author suggests that there are six nested, thus layered, sense-giving contextures [Ger. *Sinnzusammenhang*]. Before attending to these six contextures, the notion of contexture requires some elaboration.

The Sense-giving Contexture

Readers will be familiar with the idea of figure–ground relation. Consider the drawing in Fig. 2.2. When such figures are shown to participants in psychological research, most report seeing a white Maltese cross, whereas fewer see a black cross oriented along the diagonals with triangular ends. Still fewer yet see something else, for example, a (circus) tent viewed from above. Now it is still the same drawing, yet different figures are seen. It is important to retain that seeing these different things is not the result of different interpretations, because for an interpretation to occur, something needs to be given in the first place. In the present instance, given is whatever you see. The different figures are the result of different figure–ground constellations of the *same* drawing. When the figure changes, so does the ground; and if the ground is changed, so is the figure. The two are mutually constitutive, and together they make the whole. Psychologically, however, the figure is salient whereas the ground recedes to the point of becoming unnoticed. The whole we refer to here as a contexture. As a whole, it makes sense. In addition, it also

Fig. 2.2 The drawing allows different figure–ground constellations. Depending on how you gaze, the dominant figure may be a white Maltese cross or a black cross along the diagonals. Some may also see something like a square circus tent viewed from above.

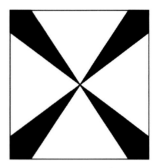

gives sense to whatever figure stands out, for the contexture determines the ground, which is everything from the contexture that is not included in the figure.

We suggest that Vygotsky's notion of a layered sense-giving field can be understood in terms of six nested, sense-giving contextures: (a) the lived world indicated by the sign; (b) the system of signs (e.g. language); (c) the sign as an expressive act; (d) the sign as a communicative act; (e) the communicative act as a solicitation of behavior; and (f) the in-order-to motive, which makes intelligible the *now, here,* and *thus* of the communicative act. In the following, we describe and discuss each of these contextures using an instant from the life of a split sixth- and seventh-grade elementary classroom (Fig. 2.3). During the recess between the two periods of science, the teacher had set up a tug of war but included a block and tackle that favored his side of the rope by a factor of 5:1. The teacher won the contest even though the students eventually amounted to 20 and included a peer, who had jammed the breaks on his wheelchair. The teacher then invited students to a discussion why they lost even though they were in the majority. Because it was difficult to understand the arguments, the teacher invited student speakers to the chalkboard and make drawings to accompany their verbal explanations; one of these students was Shamir (Fig. 2.4).

The Lived World Indicated by the Sign

A sign generally and a word as a particular sign specifically *makes sense* when it brings into the *accented* visible a particular aspect of the surrounding world; but it may also refer to ideal things, which, nevertheless, are as real for communication participants as the things that they see. When the teacher in the lesson fragment (Fig. 2.4) uses the word "end" in asking, "which end do I pull?," the word makes immediately sense because there are different parts of the drawn pulley system where the teacher could pull. The "end" thus signifies something in a world that is common to the senses of the two participants as much as to all the members of this class, the second teacher, and the research team present in the room. In the same way, both use the term "banister," and using the word makes sense because in the preceding part of the whole-class conversation, the horizontal line with hatches

Fig. 2.3 A scene from an elementary classroom where 20 students are engaged in a tug of war against their science teacher (in doorway), who had "rigged" the competition in his favor using a block and tackle. The inclination of the students' bodies give a sense of the effort they make to win against their teacher.

below has been used to signify the presence and location of a banister to which one part of the pulley is attached. This aspect of sense is the one that the term "meaning" normally denotes: "meaning" is the thing or idea that the word signifies. The word itself is the signifier. Readers may already notice that the participants are talking about the tug of war that has happened before; and the configuration of pulley (system) and ropes—or rather an alternative to it—is signified in the drawing. This drawing also makes sense because it renders visible some aspects of a recent passed that all those present in the room have lived through. The drawing consists not of words but of chalk lines. It is an assembly of lines with specific shapes that constitute a set of signs making present a not-so-distant past—or, here, an alternative to that situation where the students lost the competition. Thus, argumentation may unfold in part in the form of signs other than words. These other signs include drawings and hand gestures. This is so, as we can see, in the depicted lesson fragment, for when the teacher asks, "Where do I pull?," Shamir moves his hand along the line signifying a rope connecting the center of the pull and the banister.

Here we note that the "*word* makes sense." We do not write, the student or teacher makes sense of the word. Here, the grammatical structure of the phrase

Fig. 2.4 A scene from the whole-class discussion where the students and teacher are engaged in an argumentation about why the 20 students had lost the tug of war. Here, Shamir presents the design of a competition that he proposes would no longer favor the teacher.

changes the nature of the agent, which is no longer a human being but language (a part thereof). This opens up a question that requires more thorough investigation: What do students or teachers really do when they are said to "make sense" or "make meaning" of a word or phrase? (chapter 7). A word or phrase makes sense because it fits into and has a place in the totality of a world, here the one shared by the participants. The "end" and the "banister" are perceptually accessible as features in this world—markings on the chalkboard. These features are common to their senses and also are common sense. The word banister does signify a feature in the pulley system, which in turn signifies a feature in the world they inhabit and that everyone present was able to see behind the teacher while they were part of the tug of war (Fig. 2.3). That is, the words and phrases make sense because the participants already *know their way around that part of the world* that the former designate and signify. This is precisely the conclusion pragmatic philosophers have come to when investigating what it takes to be able to interpret a language. Thus, in the limit it is impossible to distinguish a difference between knowing a language and knowing one's way around the world. Much earlier, Vygotsky (1987) had come to the same conclusion near the end of his life when he writes—in the final chapter of his rather heterogeneous *Thinking and Speech*—that "the sense of the word depends on one's understanding of the world" (p. 276). It is the word that *absorbs* its "intellectual and affective content from the entire context in which it is intertwined" (p. 276). Vygotsky thus comes to the conclusion that there is a "prevalence of sense over meaning, of the phrase over the word, and of the whole context over the phrase," and this prevalence is "the rule rather than the exception" not only in external but also in inner speech (p. 277).

We can therefore say that if there were an interpretation of text involved, which explicates the text in some way, always and already presupposes a practical comprehension of the world; and this practical understanding initiates, accompanies, and concludes the interpretive endeavor (Ricœur 1986). But, and this is important for understanding the phenomenon of argumentation, existing practical comprehension of the world is developed and enhanced by the explication that the interpretive endeavor produces.

One pragmatic philosopher is quite adamant about the need for the term "meaning" (Wittgenstein 1953/1997). Wittgenstein not only suggests that there is no place for this concept in a pragmatic philosophy of language but also that this "philosophical concept has its place in a primitive idea of the way language functions," though "one can also say that it is the idea of a language more primitive than ours" (p. 3). The philosopher proposes instead to focusing on how language is used, that language-use *is* its meaning. In the present situation, for example, the two adversaries orient toward something where it makes sense to use the verb "pull" and where there is a banister present (Fig. 2.4). They both use the terms and, in so doing, get their attendant business done: a science lesson about the function of pulleys. The depth of this statement becomes more salient as we describe the other sense-giving contextures.

There is more that we need to consider here to get at the function of language in a speech situation—which, to anticipate, is the model and ontogenetic origin of any written communicative form. That is, we need to consider the relation between the signifier and the signified. Let us begin with the phenomenon that goes under the name of *pointing*, technically referred to as *deictic gesture* when it involves some movement of the body. In the lesson fragment, Shamir's hand moves along the line the drawing that connects the pulley with the banister (Fig. 2.4). Why would one say that he is pointing? The answer is that he is pointing because there is something to be pointed to: the line representing the rope where the teacher is to pull in the proposed configuration of the tug of war. The already existing line, perceivable to all and to their commonsense vision, *motivates* the hand movement. But this line stands out, is figure against ground, because of the hand in its direction and moving along in what is commonly referred to as an *iconic gesture*. It is called iconic because of the perceptual similarity between the direction of the line and the direction of the movement. These considerations thus exhibit the mutually constitutive nature of the pointing gesture and the thing pointed to. If there was nothing obviously in the direction of the hand-arm configuration or the movement of the hand, then the designated recipient of the speech might ask, "Are you trying to show me something?" Or, when one person is taken to be gazing intently toward something—the result of the particulars of the bodily configuration in that situation—

the other might ask, "What are you looking at?" The answer may indeed be: "Nothing in particular."

This analysis may now be extended to words, which, in human evolution, came later than the body configurations that served as the earliest of sign forms. The use of the term "banister" makes sense because something in their common world constitutes a physical banister, but the banister comes to be figure in this instant because of the word. Just as in the case of pointing, there is a mutually constitutive relation between naming and thing. The word *bannister* is naming (pointing to, highlighting) because there already is a thing available in the speech situation, which motivates the naming; but the thing is present and highlighted only because of the naming. This leads us to the concept that Vygotsky was heading toward, that is, to the idea of a "sense-giving field, different from the visible," which constitutes "an accented visible" (El'konin 1994, p. 23). There is thus a visible field, which, in our lesson fragment, is the pulley system drawn on the chalkboard. The language in the fragment has the function to make some aspects stand out, such as the end where the teacher is to be pulling or the location of the banister. In a different literature consistent with this analysis, the phenomenon has been discussed in terms of the Aristotelian idea of the apophantic function of language (Heidegger 1977). Thus, a statement (Gr. *apophansis*) lets something *be seen* (Gr. *phainô*) *from itself* (Gr. *apó*). This definition is apparent from the preceding discussion, because the "banister," for example, already has given itself to be seen. What language does is nothing other than allowing this already given line, standing for the banister, become figure and stand out against everything else as the ground. *Letting something*—i.e. that which speech is about—*be seen from itself* is one fundamental function of language; another function, soliciting behavior from another, constitutes another.

Visibility is produced not only by naming things. In the case of emphases, produced by varying speech intensity, intonation, and other means, particular parts of speech come to be made to stand out. These means are resources for limiting the range of things that words and phrases are to bring to the fore. In the teacher question "Wh*ich* end do I pull?," part of the interrogative is emphasized. By asking for a specific end—one of the various parts in the system where a pull can be effected—the phrase makes visible that there are multiple possible ends. Emphasis on the interrogative is a resource for orienting to one or another part of the pulley system. Indeed, the first question "Where do I pull?" would allow the pulling to occur anywhere in the system, not just on one of the ropes. The phrase "Which end do I pull?" selects among the possible parts, and, thus, makes those pieces of the world stand out that can be seen as "ends." These ends are not the important part of the request. The question is not about the ends but rather about *which* of these different ends the teacher is supposed to pull on.

The System of Signs

Words make sense because they are part of a system of words, that is, they are constitutive parts of language. If someone asked "What is a banister?," then the reply might be something like this: "A handrail used along a set of stairs or around a deck together with its supporting structure." Now, instead of one word, we have a series of word making a definition. This series consists of words, all of which again are constitutive of language. In reply to the definition, the first person may now ask, "But what do you mean by 'handrail'?" or "What do you mean by 'supporting structure'?" Take the former case to which the reply might be, "A handrail is a rail fixed on supporting posts intended to be grasped by the hand to gain support or safety." Readers certainly anticipate at this point that this "game" could go on ad infinitum or, more likely, to the point that the second person becomes exasperated and annoyed, asking something like "What is wrong with you today, don't know you what I mean?" or "Isn't it common sense what I mean?" This is precisely what has happened in sociology courses that H. Garfinkel (1967) taught and where he gave the following assignment: Record an everyday exchange and then write in the left of two columns; in the right column next to each phrase write what the speakers understood and were talking about. Although the students quickly completed a first version of the assignment, their task became increasingly difficult and laborious when the instructor requested more accuracy, clarity, and distinctness. When the instructor suggested that he would only know what the participants in the exchange talked about from reading what the students wrote literally in the right column, "they gave up with the complaint that the task was impossible" (p. 26). Vygotsky (1987) actually intuited that this would be the case, which led him to write: "We never know the complete sense of anything, including that of a given word. The word is an inexhaustible source of new problems. Its sense is never complete" (p. 276). No wonder, then, that Garfinkel's students were struggling and characterizing the task as impossible.

Here we see two important aspects of the way in which language works. First, any word can be explicated using other words, which is the result of language constituting a system in which each word is connected to other words. If there were indeed something like words that are not part of the language—an inherent contradiction—then it would not be a word at all. At the very instant that some sound-word has a function in an exchange it inherently is part of the shared language and thus may be explicated in other words. The first time one person said to another "I am going to google this word," and the other person says something, "so what did you find," the verb has had a function and can be explicated in terms of a subset of the existing language—even if the word had never been used before (e.g. Roth 2013). Second, Garfinkel's students noted that the task was impossible. The task is impossible because language does not just stand on its own. It is an integral feature of life generally and of human activity specifically. In the philosophy of language, the ensemble of language and the practical activity to which it belongs is referred to as *language-game* (Wittgenstein 1953/1997). That is, this term does not refer to language as a game, though it may be seen or function as such (e.g. as in the concept of *discourse*). Instead, it is life activity as a whole, including its practical part and associated language. When the teacher says, "Where do I pull?" (Fig. 2.4), then he is not so much making a statement about the world but doing something as part of the ongoing lesson (see below). The ensemble of language and activity also has been theorized in cultural-historical activity theory—activity referring to a societally motivated form of collective process that satisfies some need—which consists of practical activity together with speech activity (Leont'ev 1971). In Vygotsky's approach, the equivalent would be an ensemble consisting of the world accessible to the senses, a cultural field, and language, which is conceived of as a sense-giving field that accents what is accessible and thereby makes it figure.

Sign-use as an Expressive Act

Speaking and any other form of sign-use is a form of expression, which stands alongside other forms of expressions, such as doing something. Any form of action, even non-action, can be taken as expressing something or some intention. This is so even if the person is seen as not acting at all, as in "Look, he is doing nothing" or, as happened at the end of Shamir's presentation, "But then Doctor Roth doesn't have anything to pull at." Not pulling also is a form of action the initiative of which may be attributed to a person. In the lesson fragment, after the teacher ends, Shamir immediately begins to speak. That is, he acts; and he does so independent of any content that his speech might articulate. The teacher also acts, as shown above, in not contesting the speaking floor and, as the next turns show, in attending to and receiving what Shamir is saying. This non-acting is significant, because it does give the student the metaphorical space and time to articulate his case. The teacher thus may be said to provide this student with space for expressing himself; in so doing, his actions also manifest a particular teacher orientation to science classroom talk. This latter aspect is particularly salient when a long, 3.8-second pause is developing. In doing nothing, the teacher actually does something: he contributes to making space and time for the student to continue, which Shamir does in taking a new start at the articulation of a system including a pulley system that would not have given the teacher an advantage. The pause stands out in the face of the aforementioned maximum one-second silences in conversations generally and the 0.8-second silences common to teacher-student exchanges. The pause also can be seen as an expression of Shamir taken his time to continue; he is making and taking time to reformulate a reply. Even though neither speaks during the silence, and both gaze at the chalkboard, they are expressing something that everyone present can sense. The silence will have made sense because, on the one hand, it has allowed Shamir to gather and try again, and, on the other hand, it manifests the competence of a teacher who contributes student development of argumentation competence.

Sign-use as a Communicative Act

Sign-use may be an expressive act without having to communicate in the sense of letting something be known. People talk to themselves while doing something without others present; in such instances, when others are present, they actually may be confused about the function of the talk. Thus, we may hear something like, "Are you talking to me?" or "Are you trying to tell me something?" When Shamir says, "You can pull on here," while moving his hand along one of the lines signifying the ropes of a pulley system, then he communicates something not yet known on the part of his interlocutor or the audience, something that he makes known in and through speaking and pointing. In the phrase "Where do I pull?," which we hear as a question, the teacher not only solicits a reply that makes something known (see next section) but also expresses—confirmed in the light of the fact that he does not subsequently evaluate the student reply—that he does not know whatever the question is about. In doing what it is intended to do, the phrase *also* communicates something about the (psychological) state of the person articulating it. A related case exists in the use of the contrastive "but" in "but we have the banister there." Here, a contrast or contradiction is made visible. It exists in the fact that Shamir begins talking about a new banister when in fact the situation already is depicted, right where the teacher is placing his hand while saying "here" in "but we have the banister here." The phrase makes known the fact that the banister already is present and that there is no need to introduce a new one. The phrase makes sense because it makes something visible in the world, which itself makes sense because of our practical comprehension thereof (our knowledgeable way-finding in it). It makes sense and thus is intelligible.

One important form of communicative act is referred to as *formulating*. In formulating, social actors make visible what is currently going on. It is a way of coordinating social acting and orienting participants to the setting in doing what they do together. Thus, immediately following the tug of war, the teacher says, "Okay, what happened here?" But the videotape reveals a lot of noise and chatter. After a little while, the teacher says, "Now it's my turn to speak up here, and I want to select speakers rather than having conversations go on all over here." In this phrase, the current situation is formulated as "having conversations go on all over here." Everyone can hear the noise, and in one sense the teacher phrase is stating only what is common sense. What the phrase does, according to the preceding analyses, is to make the noise stand out to become figure. Although the phrase simply articulates what is available to everyone's senses, it is significant by the very fact that it states the obvious (see below). If whatever the statement says were to go without saying, the latter would not occur. Formulating thus makes visible specific forms of social order, and it does so for specific purposes, which include the *in-order-to motives* analyzed below. But formulating also occurs in this instance in the context of another formulation—here the social process that is to occur in the imminent future: "Now it's my turn to speak up here, and I want to select speakers." Formulated here is a future social action, whereby one person speaks and selects the next speaker. The teacher does not actually speak a lot, but articulates a phrase treated as a question and, in naming a student, both selects the next speaker and thereby follows the pattern of social process formulated immediately before. Formulating social actions thus stands besides naming things in the surrounding world as discussed above.

We may understand formulating to occur even if the social process is not directly named. Thus, for example, when Shamir says, "okay" (Fig. 2.4), he also marks that something is forthcoming. This may be one of the signs to which may be attributed, after the fact, the *because motive* for the long silence that follows. It lets others and the teacher in particular know that the speaker is not yet done. At that instant, the word has the in-order-to motive to ask for and create space to recollect and then continue in making the argument. The final turn of the lesson fragment begins with the contrastive "but," which formulates that what comes is to be heard as contrast to what has been heard immediately before. Thus, people do not just engage in argumentation, as if mobilizing pieces of process. Argumentation is a social endeavor, a social and collective behavior. As such, it does not just happen. It is produced in the *collective* (social) work of the participant. To make it happen, parts of the social endeavor need to be made visible. The talk, which realizes argumentation, also makes visible the very features of the work that has argumentation as its effect (outcome).

The Communicative Act as Soliciting a Behavior

In talking, we do not only communicate to make something known. A statement (phrase) makes sense because it solicits a behavior on the part of the recipient; in the articulation of the next turn, the recipient in turn affirms and produces the initiated social transaction. Without difficult and without having to do whatsoever interpretation, we can hear the teacher ask a question, "Where do I pull? Wh*ich* end do I pull?" Questions (are intended to) initiate a reply. In the present instance, the phrase "You can pull on *here*" follows the preceding "Where do I pull? Wh*ich* end do I pull?" There are other forms of solicited behavior, such as when students follow the instructions of a teacher. The above-discussed case of the teacher stating "Now it's my turn to speak up here, and I want to select speakers," may be heard as an instruction, which students follow in becoming quiet and attending to what the teacher says next. Making an invitation solicits a reply, which may come in the form of accepting (preferred) or a declining the invitation (non-preferred).

Statements may not be intended by the speaker to solicit a behavior but do so nevertheless. When Shamir begins anew in stating his case, saying "*this* is a banister," the teacher immediately replies, "but we have the banister here." In this situation, a statement has solicited a counter-statement. It is precisely this phenomenon that is at heart of the dialogical approach to language, whereby the "attitude toward the other's consciousness a peculiar *perpetuum mobile* is achieved," "an endless dialogue where one reply begets another, which begets a third, and so on to infinity" (Bakhtin 1984, p. 230).

All speech implies its own intelligibility. In addressing someone else, whatever the in-order-to motive, speakers imply the intelligibility of the saying; and recipients, too, orient to the intelligibility of the said. Even when the content of the speech may appear contradictory, recipients orient such that they find a way so that the content is intelligible (Garfinkel 1967). Importantly, in soliciting a specific behavior, the speaker (consciously, unconsciously, or non-consciously) takes into account the other. We do not have to think about how we ask a question but we adapt it to the intended recipient. A question will differ when talking to a child than to a partner, which may differ again from the question about the same topic that we might ask a stranger (e.g. on an airplane) or a colleague. Even if speakers do not think about the recipient, about how the recipient might hear what the former are saying, they still phrase the statement such that the intended behavior is more likely than any other one.

The In-order-to Motive and the Now, Here, *and* Thus *of the Communicative Act*

The most encompassing contexture Schütz (1932) articulates is the *in-order-to motive*, which constitutes intelligibility of the *now, here,* and *thus* of a word or phrase. Consider the following alternative exchange between Shamir and his teacher. If instead of saying "but *this* is the banister," the teacher had said, with rising intonation, "a banister?," which makes it hearable as a question, the reply might have been an affirmation, "yea, a banister" (turn 3). In such a situation, the phrase is taken as questioning the thing, and the affirmation constitutes the thing to be indeed a banister.

Fragment 2.2
 1 S: *this* is a banister.
 2 T: a banister?
 3 S: yea, a banister.

The exchange could have been different, where turn 2 again is treated as a question concerning the nature of the thing, and the reply now retracts "banister" and offers "railing" as the alternative category. The question makes sense because it initiates a reconsideration and the articulation of an alternative concept.

Fragment 2.3
 1 S: *this* is a banister.
 2 T: a banister?
 3 S: oh no, a railing.

There are still other possibilities for the exchange to take place. In Fragment 2.4, a counter-question follows the question. Indeed, turn 3 formulates turn 2 as a (critical) questioning of the word used. But while so doing, it offers up a query in turn concerning the in-order-to motive. That is, the phrase also marks that the apparent question does not make sense now, here, and thus, for the line as representing the banister along the stairs and platform leading to the classroom is common sense.

Fragment 2.4
  1 S: *this* is a banister.
  2 T: a banister?
  3 S: yea, a banister. why are you asking?

The sense of a phrase is a function of the social situation in which it occurs. Thus, Fragment 2.2 in the context of an English as second language class for foreign students may be perceived as entirely appropriate, whereas in a class of native speaking students, especially when these are older, turn 2 may sound quaint, and even lead to an expansion querying its intent, as in Fragment 2.4. Important here is the linguistic competence even of these student speakers to distinguish the different situation and to reacting appropriately as the different fragments unfold.

In the opening part of the preceding section, we point to Vygotsky's realization of the limited nature of the concept of "meaning," which only designates one of an unspecified number of zones of sense. In this section, we articulate six such zones, which we denote by the term *contexture* for the purpose of marking the interplay of figure and ground that occurs when a word (sign) makes sense. Vygotsky (1987) pointed to the need of distinguishing between sense and meaning. The preceding analyses show that a word (sign) makes sense in very different contextures where it is a constitutive part. In other words, the word does very different things, and what it does makes sense because it is perceived in this or that contexture. Whereas the "meaning" of a word is limited and specified by the definition/s that appear/s in a dictionary, "the word's sense is inexhaustible" so that its "real sense is determined by everything in consciousness which is related to what the word expresses" (p. 276). The psychologist thus concludes: "ultimately, the sense of a word depends on one's understanding of the world as a whole and on the internal structure of personality" (p. 276). This should have massive consequences for science education, the ways in which we think about teaching, and the ways in which we research and interpret classroom conversations. Sense is much more important than meaning, which is only a minor aspect of language-in-use. Moreover, it is not so that humans *make* sense. Instead, the particular activities in which we engage—as teachers or students in lessons or clients and cashiers in supermarkets—constitute events from which the sense of a phrase or action derives. This is apparent in everyday situations when we say about something that *it* makes sense. That is, we thereby state that some phrase or action makes sense in the totality of the ongoing event. It is quite apparent that in this situation, word meaning may be totally irrelevant to what is going on, constituting but a carrier for other communicative aspects (e.g. Vološinov 1930; Vygotsky 1987). Thus, in one of our studies, the analysis of recordings in a physics class reveal that the word "penis" could be heard. But the male reproductive organ has nothing to do with physics. Moreover, there was no surrounding talk that would have provided any clues about the "meaning" of the word in this context. Instead, our study shows that the sound-word had to be understood as part of a (language-) game (Roth 2015). What the rules were had to be discovered in the playing of this game; and the winner of the game gained the right to begin, and determine the rules of, the next game. That is, no language and pattern teaching could prepare someone for participating in this game, because ordinary word "meanings" were not part, the discovery of which also was part of the game. That is, participants in this game had to have an intuitive sense of what was going on, where things were at, and what it took to resolve the puzzle posed in the first articulation of this for physics courses unusual word.

References

Bakhtin, M. M. (1984). *Problems of Dostoevsky's poetics*. Austin, TX: University of Texas Press.
Bateson, G. (1979). *Mind and nature: A necessary unity*. New York, NY: E. P. Dutton.
El'konin, B. D. (1994). *Vvedenie v psixologiju razvitija: B tradicii kul'turno-istoricheskoj teorii L. S. Vygotskogo* [Introduction to the psychology of development: In the tradition of the cultural-historical theory of L. S. Vygotsky]. Moscow: Trivola.
Garfinkel, H. (1967). *Studies in ethnomethodology*. Englewood Cliffs, NJ: Prentice Hall.
Heidegger, M. (1977). *Sein und Zeit* [Being and time]. Tübingen: Max Niemeyer.
Il'enkov, E. (1977). *Dialectical logic: Essays in its history and theory*. Moscow: Progress.
Leont'ev, A. A. (1971). *Sprache, Sprechen, Sprechtätigkeit* [Language, speaking, speech activity]. Stuttgart: Kohlhammer.
Marx, K., & Engels, F. (1978). *Werke band 3* [Works Vol. 3]. Berlin: Dietz.
Ricœur, P. (1986). *Du texte à l'action: Essais d'herméneutique II* [From text to action: Essays in hermeneutics, II]. Paris: Éditions du Seuil.
Roth, W.-M. (2013). Technology and science in classroom and interview talk with Swiss lower secondary school students: A Marxist sociological approach. *Cultural Studies of Science Education, 8*, 433–465.
Roth, W.-M. (2015). Meaning and the real life of language: Learning from "pathological" cases in science classrooms. *Linguistics and Education, 30*, 42–55.
Schütz, A. (1932). *Der sinnhafte Aufbau der sozialen Welt: Eine Einführung in die verstehende soziologie* [Phenomenology of the social world]. Vienna: Julius Springer.
Vološinov, V. N. (1930). *Marksizm i filosofija jazyka: osnovnye problemy sociologičeskogo metoda v nauke o jazyke* [Marxism and philosophy of language: Application of the sociological method in linguistics]. Leningrad: Priboj.
Vygotsky, L. S. (1987). *The collected works of L. S. Vygotsky* (Vol. 1). New York, NY: Springer.
Vygotsky, L. S. (1999). *The collected works of L. S. Vygotsky: Scientific legacy* (Vol. 6). New York, NY: Springer.
Wittgenstein, L. (1997). *Philosophische Untersuchungen/Philosophical investigations* (2nd ed.). Oxford: Blackwell. (First published in 1953)
Zavershneva, E. Iu. (2010a). The Vygotsky family archive: New findings—Notebooks, notes, and scientific journals of L. S. Vygotsky (1912–1934). *Journal of Russian and East European Psychology, 48*(1), 34–60.
Zavershneva, E. Iu. (2014). The problem of consciousness in Vygotsky's cultural-historical psychology. In A. Yasnitsky, R. Van der Veer, & M. Ferrari (Eds.), *The Cambridge handbook of cultural-historical psychology* (pp. 63–97). Cambridge: Cambridge University Press.

3

Children's Reasoning and Problem Solving

In everyday situations, children encounter various moments of reasoning and decision-making that lead to certain actions. For instance, a child enters the dining room and says, "I am so hungry." She looks around the kitchen table and finds an apple. She grabs it and immediately takes a big bite. Based on her observation (seeing and feeling at the moment of grabbing) of the object on the kitchen table (the context of its location), she instantly takes that this is an apple (shape, color, skin texture, weight) that may be safely eaten; and she decides to take a bite. What would she do if she were to see an object that looks like but actually was not an apple? What would happen if she were to grab it? She might feel something not quite like an apple and then would not just take a bite. Instead, she might look around and put the object into a decoration basket on the bookshelves. In that short moment, the object has made sense in this surrounding. The child's actions, including her reasoning, were immediate and spontaneous when the apple appeared real. Yet, had it not been an apple (or fake apple) on first sight, she might have started to wonder why this object was there and where it belonged. It would have required reflection and the making of connections with the surrounding situation: reasoning in this context would have become reflective.

Reflective reasoning, as sense making, requires more of the thinking process to infer relationships between phenomena and the surroundings than spontaneous reasoning. Some psychologists explain two types of reasoning—inference from intuitive reasoning and reflection on relevant knowledge of the specific situation in the discussion of thinking systems (e.g. Evans and Stanovich 2013). Intuitive thinking is fast, automatic, and spontaneous with no or little effort, including examples of reading words on billboards or biking on an empty trail. Reflective thinking is slow, effortful, and complex, such as when figuring out the origin and nature of an unexpected scene or evaluating the validity of a complex argument (Kahneman 2011). Intuitive thinking automatically and continually runs and generates suggestions for reflective thinking with impressions, intuitions, intentions, and feelings, and reflective thinking evaluates these suggestions to solve the problems of a moment. That is, even though intuitive thinking always supports reasoning and decision making, reflective thinking is necessary to evaluate ideas with working memories and reach better conclusions. Teaching for reasoning skills in science classrooms is to develop children's reflective reasoning in situations that are complex and multifaceted and therefore require children to work through their knowledge, experiences, and imagination. In the process, they go beyond the level of making a simple and intuitive statement (intuitive thinking). Children's scientific reasoning is an event as part of which certain artifacts, phenomena, and relationships come to make sense in the context of science. It thus is reflective, complex, and effortful. In this chapter, we show how children's reasoning emerges and develops through spontaneous to reflective thinking and how sense-giving contexture of problem solving was shaped and reshaped over the interaction of children and the teacher.

The Complexity of Young Children's Reasoning

Scientific reasoning has been emphasized as an essential part of scientific literacy to develop children's informed decision-making and actions. This requires careful observation, reflection and interpretation on the observed data, and evaluation on the relationship among knowledge, data, and the situation at hand. By encouraging students to reflect on and evaluate their explanation based on evidence, teachers strive to develop scientific thinking with the essence of which lies on the coordination of theories (claims, statements, etc.) and evidence (data, phenomena, information, etc.). For example, a claim may be made stating that the light source was moving from the east to the south and to the west based on the data of shadow formation. A scientific explanation develops based on the evidence, everyday experiences, data, and experiences of how the length and direction of shadow formation are related to the light sources. To accept certain theories and reject others and justify the decisions, the coordination of theories and evidence needs to be articulated. *Good* scientific reasoning involves critically examining claims with a cluster of reliable evidence, evaluating abnormal phenomenon or outliers in data sets, and analyzing the covariation between the observed (data) and the proposed claim/theory for a better explanation to the problems.

As children move through several developmental stages, their participation in reasoning is expected to develop. Secondary students tend to be expected to participate in forms of reasoning and problem solving that may be characterized as more advanced than what young children participate in. This is so particularly in terms of their sophistication of data examination and interpretation and coordination with different claims, hypothesis, and theories that they and their peers might generate. Yet, young children do demonstrate the covariation of events as an indicator of causality and discriminate indeterminate situations from determinate ones in relational reasoning (Schulz et al. 2008) and process relation-based (correlations among variables and cause and effect) and model-based (theoretical models beyond observation or variables) reasoning (Metz 2011). Children are indeed capable

Fig. 3.1 Introducing the mystery object

of reasoning and participating in activities such that the relationship between phenomena and the surroundings make sense. This means, reasoning in science classrooms is reflective and relational, which goes beyond spontaneous and intuitive reasoning. How do children develop to the point where relational and reflective thinking may be ascribed to them as higher cognitive function? How are they socially and cognitively engaged in reasoning when they encounter problem-solving contexts? What pedagogical efforts could develop children's scientific reasoning which is more reflective, relational, and complex than everyday spontaneous reasoning? The following example exhibits a case of the complexity of children's spontaneous and reflective reasoning in a science classroom composed of second- and third-grade students. This classroom episode showcases the emergence and development of children's reasoning through social interactions and also the challenges of going beyond spontaneous intuitive reasoning in science problem solving.

A classroom teacher designed a problem solving activity to encourage students to learn how to make a claim based on observation as curriculum goals. She intended to develop children's observation and reasoning skills throughout a problem solving process. By introducing a mystery object, she invites children to make a claim, observe, and justify their claims. At the beginning of the science lesson, the teacher brings out a basket of mystery objects, addressing the children that she has a mystery for them (Fragment 3.1a, Fig. 3.1).

Fragment 3.1a
 1 T: I have a mystery for you guys today. So here you go, I'm gonna give you all something that looks like this. Look at that, and I'm not gonna tell you what it is.
 2 C: I know what it is.

3 Ss: onion. onions.

She makes the statement that she has a mystery object and she is not going to tell them what it is (turn 1). Yet, even before she completed her turn to introduce the activity, children immediately respond: that's "onion." Carter, without hesitation says he knows what it is (turn 2) and others say that's an onion (turn 3). The mystery object looked like an onion, as it had brownish, thin, and dry peeling skin and a round shape like onion. Even though the size was like a ping-pong ball, a lot smaller than onions normally seen in the market, the look of it was very similar to onion. At the first glimpse of the mystery object, children did not have to interpret the object: it was giving itself as an onion. The children could not help but see an onion in the same way as a physicist participating in another research project said she could not help but see a slope where in fact she needed to look at the abscissa values of a mathematical function (Roth 2015). The children drew on commonsense reasoning, which is immediate and spontaneous, and makes a lot of good sense. At the very moment children perceive the object, it no longer is a mystery object. The teacher asks children not to share their ideas out loud with others and to think about other possible claims.

Fragment 3.1b
4 T: okay well if you know then just keep it to yourself. um. so, you are going to first of all make a guess as to what it is.
5 C: I know what it is.
6 T: okay. keep it to yourself, keep it to yourself! so the question of the day is, what is it. and you have to make a claim first. so you have to say I think it is … whatever. okay? maybe it's an onion, maybe it's a hat. for a very small headed person.
7 C: you said what it is.
8 T: sorry. okay.
9 A: I was just gonna guess that.
10 T: and so when you cut it apart you're gonna come up with what you think is inside of it, if it looks familiar like anything else you've cut apart.

The teacher asks children to guess what the object is. But in this situation, the children already know it is an onion because they perceive it as such. It is common to their senses and thus common sense. Merely looking at the object provides incontrovertible evidence for its classification. Their statements do not reflect hesitation. This scene shows how children's reasoning started at the very moment that the object was introduced as mystery object and children looked at it. Their reasoning was spontaneously spread and shared over the object and the word, "onion" in the context of mystery. The mystery no longer was mysterious. Yet, the teacher knew that the mystery object was not an onion but a tulip blub. She chose this object to emphasize children's skills of looking for evidence to make and justify their claim, and thus it was an effective artifact to pursue her curriculum goals. As the classroom dialogue develops, children's spontaneous reasoning is evident as more children state that they also propose onion (e.g. turn 9). To encourage children to think further, further examination and reflection on the mystery object was suggested such as cutting it apart and using loupes to look into it. Children go back to their small groups and start to observe the object more carefully. Yet, throughout their small group conversations the onion claim was becoming more dominant and assured. Even though the teacher kept telling the children it might not be an onion and think about something else, children did not give up their claim, onion. The onion claim was prevalent and was becoming the right answer (Fragment 3.2a). Carter even added another piece of evidence: it made his eyes water [like onion] (turn 3). Even though the teacher disapproved the evidence (turns 4 and 6), Carter explains that the teacher was wearing glasses and that is why it did not make her eyes water (turn 7). The teacher takes off her glasses and says it still does not make the eyes water; but the children do not take to this statement as evidence (turns 9 to 11). They write down onion as their claim. As the onion nature of the object was supported by more evidence, the classroom talk moved toward settling the issue. Rather than relational and reflective science thinking, children's conclusion are drawn from the immediate perception.

Fragment 3.2a
1 A: I am pretty sure it's onion but just to be a case, someone else to say it's not
2 T: I will tell you that I wouldn't have said onion if that were what it is. okay? I wouldn't tell you that. It would ruin the mystery.
3 C: yes, you would. I know what it is because it make my eyes water.
4 T: it made your eyes water, really?
5 S: what?
6 T: it doesn't make my eyes water.
7 C: that's because you have glasses on.
8 T: okay, I have glasses on. ((*She takes out her glasses and putting the object closer to her eyes.*)) No it does not make my eyes water. okay. write down your claim on. Tom, write down your claim.
9 C: so what now! because this is an onion...
10 K: yup, Carter, I think you might be right.
11 C: I, I, I thought it was an onion before she said, before she actually said it was an onion.
12 T: yeah, I was gonna guess an onion also. it's so interesting.

As the teacher continuously puts the object back to mystery and children attempt to solve the mystery with an answer, reasoning and problem solving process emerge and are experienced as collective social actions. The teacher invites children to observe and think further more critically about their conclusion. The children observe the object while peeling off skin, cutting into the object, and reporting on a milky and sticky juice, the inner texture, and a pointy part on the top. They variously describe its shape as a pumpkin, dragon fruit, dried pineapple, nut, and cabbage, thereby responding to the teacher's suggestion. But the talk remains centered on the idea of onion.

Fig. 3.2 Observing and discussing in a small group

Then the following exchange takes place in one small group (Fragment 3.2b, Fig. 3.2).

Fragment 3.2b
13 A: supposedly onion, or some kind of nut.
14 C: it's either an onion or cabbage.
15 S: cabbage?
16 C: probably an onion because it made me cry, but
17 A: that made me cry and I'm wearing glasses ... for some reason it doesn't affect some people.
18 C: I think it's like, well, I think it was making ((*chopping*))
19 A: maybe it's some type of nut, it could.
20 C: eew, that looks like peeled old pineapple ((he is showing the piece he just took out of the object)).
21 A: no, I don't think it's a pineapple.
22 C: oh my god! It smells so bad! ... and it gets into your eyes, and ... ((*he starts rubbing his eyes*)) definitely onion. these are onions or cabbage.
23 J: a cabbage? how?
24 C: look at this.
25 J: how do you feel?
26 C: I think this onion feels nice.

In the exchange, watery eyes and feel supported the claim that the mystery object was an onion. The statement that the object does not make eyes water, is rejected based on the observation that this would not affect some people as another justification why this could be an onion. Children see, feel, and smell onion on this object, and thus, their claim makes sense to them. As the teacher urged them to observe and think further, more reasons were added to justify existing claims. In this joint action, reasoning was pushed further away from spontaneous and immediate thinking. Even though their answers were not what the teacher expected to

Table 3.1 *The claim-evidence covariation in reasoning*

Evidence	Onion	Cabbage	Nut	Dried Pineapple
Shape	−	+	+	+
Brown skin	−	+	−	+
Thin, peeling skin	−	+	−	+
Smell	−	−	−	+
watery eyes	−	+	+	+
Texture	+	+	−	−
	YES ⬇	NO	NO	NO
Final claim	Thus, the mystery object is onion.			

hear, observation, making relations, justification were evidently experienced and developed through this interactive social relation. The following excerpt summarizes the argumentation surrounding the question whether the object makes eyes water. In the resultant joint reasoning, the onion claim makes *good* sense. This joint justifying process grounded the onion claim more firmly throughout the dialogue.

Fragment 3.2, Excerpt
  3 C: I know what it is because it make my eyes water.
  4 T: it doesn't make my eyes water.
  5 C: that's because you have glasses on.
  6 T: ((*taking out her glasses*) no. it does not make my eyes water.
…
  17 A: that made me cry and I'm wearing glasses … for some reason it doesn't affect some people.

In this session, the group compares, examines, and discusses different claims such as the mystery object being a cabbage, nut, or pineapple. Based on observation, everyday experiences and discussion, there is more evidence for the object to be an onion than anything else including that it is dried, brown, and the thin outer layer is peeling off; and the round shape makes the object appear like an onion despite its small size. That was strong and good evidence for supporting the onion claim. None of these were matching the other options. Thus, even though there are a few pieces of contradictory evidence, the onion claim could be the best answer *for now* in the public form of reasoning observable in the exchange. The sense-giving textures of the mystery object provide them enough evidence of onion.

In this classroom situation, reasoning is knowledge-based, data-based, and relational. There existed a certain degree of covariation between claim and evidence. For children, the sense-giving contexture around the mystery object gave sense to the mystery object being an onion. The teacher's doubt and rejection to "smell like onion" and "watery eyes" encouraged children to justify the onion claim rather than take another claim as they did feel the smell and watery eyes and also could not find anything better than onion (Table 3.1). Thus, the onion claim is making *more* sense in the sense-given field and confirmed with the shared agreement among children. In this process, reasoning exists *as* the relation between people and thus has the form of a collective social action.

As the exchange unfolds, the public reasoning process leads toward the conclusion that the mystery object is an onion. This, of course, was not part of the teacher's curricular intention. The episode thereby exemplifies the reasons why many teachers fear the constructivist approach to science learning, because it allows learners to arrive at factual knowledge inconsistent with scientific knowledge. But we have to ask, "Does it really matter whether children get the correct claim (answer), that is, that the mystery object is a tulip bulb?" If getting the correct answer is not the goal of this activity, what is the teacher's pedagogical concern here? An alternative curricular goal might be having students experience the processes of science, including thinking, reasoning, gathering evidence, mobilizing evidence in the course of an argument, and so on. All of these forms of scientific activity are indeed observable in the preceding exchanges.

What is Evidence?

The evaluation of claim-evidence connections has shown to be difficult. Adults and older students exhibit more critical examination of any existing data or other evidence that conflict with their claims. As a result, they generally tend to be more willing to explore alternative hypotheses. Young children often overlook conflicting data and show preference to supporting data to test hypothesis (Klahr and Dunbar 1988). Especially, children at an early age (4–5 year olds) do not recognize the difference between claim and evidence and often interchange these within the context of whole explanations. Thus, when children observe something that confounds their existing knowledge and theories their assessment of the covariation of data from their observation often becomes conflicted. In this regard, how children develop consistency and consilience between theory and evidence over the school years becomes a meaningful pedagogical question in classroom teaching. Evidence-based reasoning as a core aspect of scientific thinking and problem solving focuses on what evidence students use in the connection of premise and claims and how they evaluate and justify the relationships of claim and evidence. The evidence could be in the form of a single datum or a statement of relationships among data. When children suggest general rules governing the data in support of their claims, then this is regarded to be a high level of evidence-based reasoning. Competent evaluation of the relationship among a problem, evidence, and conclusion is an integral part to successful reasoning and problem solving.

The problem solving activity of mystery object shows the complexity of reasoning and problem solving process in lower elementary science classrooms. Through the interactive joint problem solving process, the children participants experience the making of claims, observations, collection of data, and justification of claims. Reasoning is collective, having started spontaneously but developing to be more reflective in relation to the observed data through classroom discussions. The relationship between claim and evidence is evident in the public forms of reasoning manifest in the lessons observed. However, the evaluation of evidence became a concern to this teacher. In the joint problem solving process, she projected a contradiction in children's evidence of smell and watery eyes. Yet the children did not treat this as a contradiction. By acknowledging that they could smell and feel watery eyes from the mystery object, there is talk about these as evidence in the making of claims. Pieces of evidence could be ignored and onion thereby came to stand as conclusion because all other claims were rejected through dialogues and there was no better one at the moment. In this regard, the fact that there was no onion smell and there were no watery eyes does not come to be treated as contradiction in the public forms of reasoning. Further evidence was not from careful and critical observation and reflection from the teacher's pedagogical perspectives.

As the teacher thought that the evidence of smell was critical and obvious enough to rule out the onion claim, she had not anticipated that the public discussion would be resisting to changing the claim from onion to the tulip bulb. Yet as discussion unfolded, the evidence of the smell, which resembled that of an onion, and the watering of the eyes, only strengthened the support for the onion claim rather than weakening it or ruling it out. From a traditional perspective of the role of the teacher, this result may be surprising; and it may be used to construct the teacher as having difficulties. However, a holistic perspective on classroom life recognizes the teacher as one part of a collective. The collective is a unit irreducible to its individual parts. This is why the living curriculum has its own life, one that differs from what teachers intend. In some instances, even when the students are only five years old, the entire curriculum is changed in the course of an unfolding lesson. What the teachers had intended to happen was overturned, and an originally marginal activity that a boy had initiated eventually became the dominant activity (Roth et al. 2013). Something similar was happening in the exchange over the mystery object. Even though the teacher had intended for the children to find out that the object was a tulip bulb, the trajectory of the public exchange moved away from a statement of this finding. It did so in the face of the apparently clear and incontrovertible evidence. The trajectory of the exchange is not exclusively due to the children, for, as could be seen in the fragments above, the teacher actively contributed to the exchange, and therefore contributed to its unfolding.

The onion claim was shared and supported in the public space of the exchange; the direction that the exchange was taking started to challenge the teacher. She kept attempting to re-direct the reasoning and problem solving, proposing counter evidence and indicating it might not be an onion. Some readers may think that the teacher could have directly explained to the children the knowledge of claim-evidence in the intended curriculum, that is, your evidence is wrong, this is not onion smell and therefore the object could not be an onion. But such a strategy might not have led anywhere. Indeed, it might have been perceived as the effort of a teacher to push her view *in the face of evidence to the contrary*. As noted above, even mature and experienced scientists see their data in a particular way—e.g. as supporting their theory when it was indeed contradicting it. This happened in one of our research project, where it took a major conceptual change for the scientists to see their data sources in a different way, which then allowed them to treat them as evidence in support of a different theory (Roth 2014).

In the case of the classroom we observed, the teacher chose not to tell them directly but participated in the problem solving process as a member of the classroom community. She learned that making verbal statements of what it is (not) would not convince children to change their minds as her several attempts to convince them that it might not be an onion was unsuccessful. Such learning on the part of the teacher is integral to a more symmetrical approach to the concept of the *zone of proximal learning* (Roth and Radford 2010). The concept frequently is used to explain why children learn in the presence of a teacher—essentially because this presence enables them to act in a way that is more advanced then when they work on their own. But teachers, too, learn in the exchanges with students—precisely because they participate in a single, collective, and joint effort. She had to figure out (i.e. learn) what actions would allow the exchange to take on a new direction so that the publicly available evidence was pointing away from the onion. As it was, in the face of the evidence available, the claim that the object was an onion made a lot of sense. Like the physicist quoted above, the children could not but see the mystery object as an onion. In the situation, the teacher moved to bring children's attention to testing the smell of onion as critical evidence in their claim. Her pedagogical concern was shifting from connecting claim and evidence to evaluating the quality of evidence in children's reasoning.

The following fragment took place after the several attempts to discuss smell as evidence. The claim was still present. The teacher asked children to provide better evidence to convince her, because she could not see it as onion.

Fragment 3.3a

  1 T: okay, but does this smell like an onion? does it make your eyes water like an onion?
  2 C: kind of.
  3 T: really?
  4 C: yes.
  5 T: I'm not convinced. to me, it, if the evidence isn't showing me, isn't saying onion because it's not like any … unless it's a new kind of onion I've never seen. how could we test it?
> 6 C: maybe it could be a baby onion.
> 7 A: yea, it's a baby onion.
  8 Al: um hm mm. how could we test it.

The fragment shows that the contradiction around the smell as evidence emerged again. She said the evidence did not show it onion and it's not like any onion she had seen before. As the onion claim was challenged by the absence of onion smell, more convincing evidence was required to validate the onion claim, yet, there also emerged a new possibility of a new kind of onion they had never seen in the exchange (3.3a, turn 5), that is, this mystery object could be a baby onion. A contradiction emerged in the joint space (Table 3.2) but it was temporarily resolved by the possibility of the object to be a new kind of onion, a baby onion.

REASONING AND PROBLEM SOLVING 47

Table 3.2 *The joint space of classroom reasoning*

Teacher talk	Joint space	Children talk
I'm not convinced. To me, it, if the evidence isn't showing me, isn't saying onion because it's not like any . . . unless it's a new kind of onion I've never seen.	*This is not onion based on the evidence.* *There needs better evidence.* *There could be a new kind of onion that the teacher had not seen before.*	Maybe it could be a baby onion. Yah, it's a baby onion.

The claim, even if it was changed to be about a baby onion, continues to be a publically acknowledged claim and the conversation unfolds into a discussion of the ways of resolving the contradiction of evidence to be an onion.

As the exchange continues to unfold, new possibilities arise with new descriptive evidence, such as the description of the looks of the object as resembling a pineapple (3.3b, turn 12, 15). Yet, this new claim could not resolve the contradiction of evidence, for the object did not have the pineapple smell (turn 14).

Fragment 3.3b
  9 T: you guys need to use evidence, right. does this ... are the things that really tell us it's an onion present in this thing?
 10 A: uh I just thought of a theory.
 11 T: what's your theory?
 12 Al: it might be true ... um, that, it could be a pineapple. I don't know why but it just reminded me of pineapple.
 13 T: does it smell like a pineapple?
 14 Ss: no.
 15 J: the skin looks like it.
 16 T: you know, it looks like a lot of things, some people took the skin off and some people said it looked like a little pumpkin, so yeah, it kinda does, but you know, sometimes things look like things and aren't really them, right. you need to look at all the evidence. right? so how could we figure out, how could we learn more about these things?

There is a formulation that what follows is a theory (Fragment 3.3b, turns 10 and 11). Turn 12 therefore is marked beforehand as a theory. There is then a {query | reply} turn pair to evaluate the theory with evidence, the smell, in which the theory comes to be negated. The contradiction of smell as evidence now was back in the public space. But this does not significantly change the line of argument. There are {invitation | acceptance} turn pairs that lead to the production of new proposals for solving the problem.

Fragment 3.3c
 17 Al: by cutting them.

18 C: hey, here is the thing. to know what it is, we go to shop, find an onion, cut it up and see what it looks like.
19 J: here is my idea. so we could open this one and we'll get a real onion that we know is an onion, and we'll cut that one open, to see if the inside is the exact same thing.
20 T: okay. so we could compare it to something that we know is an onion. do you guys agree that would be a good experiment to do?
21 Ss: yea.
22 T: what other ways can we learn more?
> 23 Al: we let it grow to see what plant comes. we can probably find it out.

Based on evidence, the onion claim was challenged, but the change to a baby onion still affirmed the onion claim. The evidence of smell was brought several times in the dialogical exchanges, yet, was not taken as critical evidence to weaken or rule out the onion claim in class. Encountering this continuous challenge, the teacher continued to participate in the dialogue as a member of problem solving community, not as an authoritarian figure of knowledge holder to give out the answers to students. She had to participate in argumentation talk to convince children that it was not onion with her own evidence (no smell of onion). Yet, the contradiction around the evidence of onion that the teacher raised was not fully taken by children and classroom problem solving was not developed the way as intended in the curriculum. The teacher agrees to children's suggestions to compare the objects and move forward the problem solving.

For the next science class, the teacher brought a cabbage and an onion, which were the two most compelling claims and compared them with the mystery object. The teacher cut the mystery object half. A child who was absent during the preceding lesson asks if it is garlic (Fragment 3.4a, turn 1).

Fragment 3.4a
1 D: is it garlic?
2 T: we wanna figure out something, we need to find evidence. so we were having a hard time finding evidence for some of the hypotheses you guys came up with the other day. right? so, so, we know that with garlic, a big piece of evidence would be what? you just said.
3 Al: the smell.
4 T: the smell, right? whether or not you consider it an unpleasant smell or a pleasant smell, it has a very strong smell, right? so. even if it's dried out, it would still have quite a strong smell. (*Walks around class letting everyone smell the mystery object*.)

5 To: ugh!
6 T: does that smell like garlic to you? anybody know what garlic smells like?

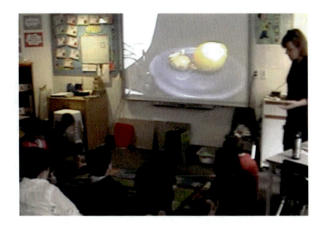

Fig. 3.3 Observing the mystery object and onion together

7 D: I know– that is definitely not garlic. it kinda, it smells like on a level of one to ten, I'd say it's a two.
8 T: okay, so what does the evidence tell you?
9 D: it's not garlic.

Then the teacher and children reviewed what they discussed about the object and put them on the visual presenter to observe them further (Figure 3.3).

The children and teacher checked the brownish skin, round shape with a pointy top that looked like an onion. Then there is an {invitation | acceptance} sequence asking for and providing really good evidence. More evidence is articulated: there are rings when you cut it half horizontally.

Fragment 3.4b

10 E: um hm, I, uh, um, cut open an onion, usually there's a variety of rings on it.
11 T: that's a good point,
12 E: so you could do that, or you could dissect it and figure out, and figure out if it has the same parts
13 T: okay, good idea. I don't have enough onions for everybody to do it, how about I'll do it, I'll cut it, we'll look at it, and see– he mentioned rings, so yes, onions do have rings in it. if this is a little onion then it should have rings as well, right?
14 D: and it should make you cry.
15 T: and it should have that strong smell, right? what do you guys think?
16 Ss: yea.

17	T:	do you agree? so, do you want me to do some cutting? and then I'll bring it around for you guys to smell? so I'm gonna cut across– oh, and look, he was talking about rings.
18	C:	yea.
19	L:	rings.

In this exchange, the mystery object is recognized to have neither distinctive rings nor onion smell. This ruled out the onion claim. In the same way, this also ruled out cabbage. The evaluation between claim and evidence was processed. In the public forum, and *as* the social relation, evidence came to be connected to claims.

Yet, the nature of the object remained a mystery. These pieces of evidence, no smell and no rings were enough to falsify claims of onion, cabbage, pineapples, garlic, and so on but could not answer what the mystery object really was. The conclusion, the mystery objects were not any of those took the whole class back to the original question, "what is this mystery object?" A new approach to the question was required to solve the current problem. The exchanges brought about the review of ideas of the different parts of plants: stem, leaves, and roots, and observed the bottom part of the mystery object where there were little nubs out. The option of planting to see what it was became a topic in the earlier exchange (Fragment 3.3c). There was some agreement to plant the objects to know more information about the mystery. A few weeks later, children saw the plant growing and it was not an onion but tulip. This makes more sense! The class later reflected on this activity as a hard lesson. In the conversation with the researcher, the teacher later stated that it was very challenging to convince children that it could be something else, not onion and she did not want to tell them what it was until they could plant the bulbs and see what grows out of it.

Evidence in Nested Sense-giving Contexture

Understanding the interplay of {claim | evidence | evaluation} and the roles of evidence is crucial for children's scientific thinking and reasoning; yet it is not an easy concept and skill for children to learn and practice. How do they understand the importance of evidence in knowledge justification and evaluation? How do they know some evidence is better and stronger than others? The dynamics of the interplay of {claim | evidence | evaluation} can only be experienced and learned in the joint realm of dialogical problem solving where different knowledge, claims, evidence, and experiences co-exist, conflict, and need to be worked out. When children participate in dialogical problem solving, often with the teacher, a joint intellectual realm of learning emerges with new ideas. For instance, in the joint space of problem solving, dialogical prompts such as "let's look for evidence," "what is your evidence to this claim?," or "I am convinced with this" invite members of problem solving community to think about what evidence means and what is required to convince others. Through the exchange of requesting and providing evidence, children experience, practice and learn the interplay of {claim | evidence | evaluation} and roles of evidence in problem solving. In the episode of mystery object, the long sustaining conflict of children's onion claim prompted the urgency of collective understanding of conflicting relationship of claim | evidence | evaluation and brought several turn-takings to bring the importance of "evidence" in claim making, such as "I have this as evidence" or "that's really good evidence." The word, "evidence" was repeatedly shared and referred in the context of claim | evidence | evaluation and later when exchanges include queries like "do you have evidence for this?" and answers like "the skin looks like it" or "it does not have the smell." In such exchanges, the need and form of evidence emerges and is enacted. The skin and smell become the *evidence* for certain claim through children's responses to the teacher's prompt. The sense of the evidence is shared through and co-exists in this joint form of public dialogue. This realm of building shared references through joint activities where the words of the exchange *are* the consciousness for the respective other and the self (Vygotsky 1987). Inherently public consciousness is a dynamic frame of reference. All public talk is integral part of a sense-giving contexture, which is continuously re/constituted as children and the teacher think and act together in the dialogical learning environment. In this zone, the teacher takes special responsibility to keep classroom dialogues continuous and effective being attentive to children's capabilities, knowledge building and curriculum goals.

The mystery object example shows how complex and multilayered children's reasoning could be in and *as* social action and how it developed in this joint space of dialogical problem solving. Providing a problem solving activity, it was expected to develop children's scientific reasoning as curriculum goals. Children started with intuitive and spontaneous reasoning to understand what the mystery object could be and further developed a higher level of reasoning which was more reflective, thorough, and evaluative toward claim making with evidence through inherently social relations. Yet children's reasoning about the mystery object was not easily moving from spontaneous thinking which was prompted by the first look in the beginning. From the first glimpse of the object, a claim of onion was made and resistant to change over time. The sense-giving contexture made the nature of the mystery object appear obvious and convincing evidence for it to be an onion, as the collected evidence did not certainly support any of the claims suggested and onion was the most supported one. In this process, both children and the teacher were challenged by the conflict arising from the evidence. The onion claim was constantly supported and challenged by evidence and counter evidence and what was convincing to children was not to the teacher. The tension was growing in the negotiation and evaluation of claims and evidence. The lack of agreement in sense-giving contextures created tension, resistance, and frustration because the two claims (onion vs. not onion) were still alive and required for further discussion. What should be shared in the sense-giving contexture in order for children and the teacher to move forward their problem solving? What was hindering children to take the smell as possible evidence to discard their claim? As children could not describe the unknown object in their own world, i.e. tulip bulb, it might be neither possible nor meaningful to expect them to say the word, tulip bulb. With no expectation on getting the word out of children's mouth, the curriculum focus was shifting from "making a claim" to "understanding the importance of evidence" in children's reasoning by emphasizing the accuracy of evidence and the importance of evaluation. "Making sense of the smell as evidence" was standing out from the sense-giving contexture, as the teacher invited children to sense the different smells and if they still supported the onion claim. For the smell of the mystery object to make sense in a different way, the teacher suggested cutting and smell onions in class.

> Teacher: So, do you want me to do some cutting? And then I'll bring it around for you guys to smell? ... So I'm cutting the onion across.

The onion was brought closely to individual children's noses. The smell of onion was tested and accepted as evidence in subsequent reasoning. The action of cutting and smelling it added critical evidence of what onions smell like and the mystery object was missing the smell to be onion. Agreeing upon the absence of the smell and rings as evidence, the problem solving was moving toward another stage of sense-making, "the mystery object is not onion." The smell as evidence is perceived, understood, and agreed in the shared sense-giving contexture where the evidence appeared, which was purposefully and effectively developed through the joint activity of reasoning and problem solving.

For the later Vygotsky, language no longer is a tool (sign) that stands between the different subjects in the way he used to suggest, a way he renounced during the last two years preceding his death. Instead, in the verbal exchange, the language is in common, for the word is impossible for one but a real possibility for two (or more) (Vygotsky 1987). Language constitutes an accented visible, an integral part of thinking and learning. Anything stated in the public forum makes something visible, whether it is actually present, such as the mystery object and its characteristics, or absent but made present for all in and with the public use of language (e.g. naming the pineapple made experiences with pineapples present). What matters to the trajectory of the conversation is the collective as a whole. As suggested above, the contributions considered individually and on their own do not bring about a change in the direction (trajectory) of the conversation. This is so because, for example, what matters is not merely that the teacher says something specific but how something said is heard and treated. It is because each word constitutes a give (e.g. on the part of the teacher) and take (e.g. on the part of the children) that the conversation has a trajectory that none of the individuals controls. The trajectory of the conversation is a characteristic of a *collective* phenomenon, concurrently and conjointly produced by all participants. It *cannot* be reduced to any one of the participating individuals.

There is something else important to the development of argumentation and reasoning that is tied to the collective endeavor. Argumentation and reasoning are forms of behavior typical of human beings; they have not been observed among other animals. Such observations have led to the recognition that any higher form of psychological function exists in the relations specific to human society (Vygotsky 1989); they are not observed in other societies (e.g. ant, bee) even though these societies, too, exhibit behaviors that cannot be reduced to the individual specimens. From the perspective of children, these higher psychological functions, here reasoning and producing argumentation, first *are* social relations and collective behaviors before they show up as individual behaviors. From the perspective of the teacher, there is a "*renewed division into two of what had been fused in one*" (p. 58). That is, if the teacher were asked, she would observe, describe the facts, and make claims that are supported by the evidence. The ensemble of actions—observing, stating evidence, making claim—constitutes one behavior, the behavior of one individual in a particular situation. But it is not a behavior that is grounded in her subjectivity. Instead, precisely because it is recognizable as a scientifically legitimate form of behavior, it is social and cultural through and through. Moreover, the teacher at one point was a child herself. It is as part of a social relation that she participated in the collective production of the behavior before she produced it on her own. In lessons observed, this one behavior unfolded as collective behavior, as seen in the following excerpt from Fragment 3.4.

Fragment 3.4, excerpt

7 D: it kinda, it smells like on a level of one to ten, I'd say it's a two.	Observation (Evidence)
8 T: okay, so what does *the evidence* tell you?	Evidence
9 D: it's not garlic.	Claim

In considering the excerpt, readers need to keep in mind that even though a child or the teacher may have said something, what matters is the effect such a saying has had. The effect is a fact in the situation and thus also the context out of which the next action is born. Thus, all three statements in the excerpt need to be seen from the perspective of a phrase that simultaneously is in the mouth of the speaker and the ears of the listener: it belongs to both. The entire sequence from turn 7 through turn 9—"it kinda, it smells like on a level of one to ten, I'd say it's a two. Okay, so what does the evidence tell you? It's not garlic"—therefore exists for both the teacher and the child. We know it does because of the successfully completed {query | reply} sequence in turns 8 and 9. In individualistic speak, the child has heard and responded to a question. (In social speak, the participants are producing the exchange together; they cannot produce it on their own, just as one hand cannot produce a clap.) The question really existed for the child. But the same child has articulated the phrases in turns 7 and 9. So these turns, too, existed for the child. That is, the entire sequence existed for the child. It participated in the establishment of the observation-evidence-claim unit. It is thus as a social relation that this unit first existed for the child. The question whether and when it will show up in the behavior of the child acting on her own is an empirical one. But, as in the case of the teacher, it still is a social behavior, for, whenever required, it can be unfolded again and produced by a group of individuals.

This way of viewing learning has consequences for teaching. If some higher function such as scientific reasoning is to show up in the behavior of individuals, then it first has to exist for them in collective behavior. Individuals, however, do not exclusively control collective behavior. From this perspective, it comes as no surprise to observe the early developmental trajectory of the whole-class conversation. It took its course almost *despite* what the teacher and individual children said. It had a dynamic of its own. But this has consequences, for if some behavior does not come together as a collective phenomenon, it will not show up in the behavior of the children. However, because behavior is collective, the teacher alone cannot force the *renewed division into two*—though obviously she can act in ways that are more conducive to it. It is precisely in situations such as the present one that teachers learn to ask questions and contribute to classroom conversations in other ways so that the intended behavior does indeed occur in the collective (Roth and Radford 2010). Because individuals participate in the collective production of the behavior, it also exists for them individually. This is so because children can act on the actions of others only when these make sense, so that both their own actions and those of the others make sense as well. This is but another way of saying that "there is nothing *other* for us from the outset that would not be our *own. For the very existence of the mind is possible only at the borderline where there is a continual coming and going of one into the other*" (Mikhailov 2001, p. 20). Without the children talking and acting in the way they do, the teacher would not develop in the way she does. She would not be learning from experience and, thereby, would not become an *experienced* teacher capable of fostering the development of reasoning and problem solving in her classroom.

The episode of mystery object shows the complexity of children's reasoning in classroom problem solving contexts. To develop children's reasoning to be more reflective and evidence-based, opportunities of understanding a certain phenomenon with the surrounding context are required, which invite children to knowledge and evidence evaluation and negotiation in classrooms. Through this process, evidence-based reasoning becomes collective for evidence becomes evidence in {claim | evidence | evaluation} relationship only through public acceptance. Educational psychologists and researchers have examined children's scientific thinking by using various reasoning test models, and yet much research was practiced within the conditions of individual performance and knowledge in controlled problem contexts such as hypothesis testing and inductive or deductive reasoning. For instance, in some research individual students' performance, statements, and knowledge outcomes were coded to analyze what strategies students used to successfully solve problem cases (Zimmerman 2007). Yet such approach has limitations to explain the complexity of children's reasoning process in classroom situations. If children's reasoning were evaluated by such controlled approach, children's reasoning in this episode of mystery object problem solving would be evaluated as an unsuccessful case of learning as individual students did not reach a desirable conclusion as intended in the curriculum. It could be seen as only a messy process full of contradictions within different claims and forms of evidence. Yet in the episode, the complexity of theory-evidence coordination was emerging, experienced, learned and practiced with the surroundings of thoughts and actions and claim and evidence were constantly interrupted and negotiated in a shared problem space. The continuity and collectivity of reasoning as social action in classroom settings was evident and children's reasoning was developing and making sense within the sense-giving contexture as a whole. This collective and holistic dynamics of children's reasoning may not be assessed and understood by the pen-and-pencil reasoning test models.

Children's reasoning as participatory collective thinking raises pedagogical challenge of how teachers perceive and develop children's reasoning in science classrooms. In a strong sense, the teacher is part of whatever we use to evaluate "children's reasoning," for the talk includes the teacher as a recipient. It is not merely children's reasoning, but reasoning in this situation. As children's reasoning and problem solving skills have been understood and evaluated based on individuals' capacity to justify with evidence and reach correct conclusions, the complexity of collective reasoning challenges teachers' intentions and teaching practice with curriculum goals. Seen in this episode, the curriculum goal and teacher's intentions were no longer to orient children's reasoning and actions into desired directions. There was only a community of problem solvers whose ideas and experiences were intertwined, waiting for negotiation and resolution. The teacher had to give up the authority and curriculum intention to be able to forward the reasoning and problem-solving task. Being attentive and flexible with the complexity of children's evidence, creating contexts so that actions and words make sense, and participating in the conversation unfolding was essential for children's learning to emerge from the lessons. In the (collective) exchange of classroom talk, teachers are positioned as community members of thinking and reasoning, not as providers of correct knowledge, thus, their roles are to invite and participate in the exchange of thoughts and actions. They model how to claim with evidence in the conversation, require evidence, and acknowledge whenever evidence appears to emphasize the role of evidence in scientific reasoning. Being a member of problem solving community, teachers' role is no longer instructing but participating in classroom discussions with their thoughts, evidence, and claims. It requires teachers to shift the focus of teaching scientific reasoning from getting correct answers to making sense of a phenomenon in the complexity of diverse experiences and knowledge. Children learn how to reason through reasoning together with the teacher who is also reasoning together with children in a collective community.

References

Evans, J., & Stanovich, K. (2013). Dual-process theories of higher xognition: Advancing the debate. *Perspectives on Psychological Science, 8*(3), 223–241.

Kahneman, D. (2011). *Thinking, fast and slow*. New York, NY: Farrar, Straus and Giroux.

Mikhailov, F. T. (2001). The "other within" for the psychologist. *Journal of Russian and East European Psychology, 39*(1), 6–31.

Roth, W.-M. (2014). Learning in the discovery sciences: The history of a "radical" conceptual change or the scientific revolution that was not. *Journal of the Learning Sciences, 23*, 177–215.

Roth, W.-M. (2015). Becoming aware: Towards a post-constructivist theory of learning. *Learning: Research and Practice, 1*, 38–50.

Roth, W.-M., Goulart, M. I. M., & Plakitsi, K. (2013). *Science during early childhood: A cultural-historical perspective*. Dordrecht: Springer.

Roth, W.-M., & Radford, L. (2010). Re/thinking the zone of proximal development (symmetrically). *Mind, Culture, and Activity, 17*, 299–307.

Zimmerman, C. (2007). The development of scientific thinking skills in elementary and middle school. *Developmental Review, 27*, 172–223.

4

Argumentation as Joint Action

It is common to suppose that human individuals speak to place their earlier private cogitations or mental structures into the public arena. Indeed, a constructivist commitment immediately leads us to such a supposition. However, any individual person uses language that precedes her. More importantly, anything a person can say is already made possible by language, which is why "scientific misconceptions" are cultural and historical rather than individual phenomena (Roth 2008). A person, therefore, only realizes what language already has in store; and, as such, anything that can be said already exists at the collective level. Contrasting his approach to that chosen by Piaget, Vygotsky points out that children individualize the social rather than the (untamed, raw) individual being socialized into collective, cultural forms. In other word, when we talk (or write) it is language that speaks. We leave speaking to language. Such decentering of agency also occurs when Vygotsky (1989) suggests that any higher psychological function *was* a social relation first. He does not write that there is something "constructed" "in" a social relation and then internalized; instead, what was a social relation with another person later can be found as the behavior of the individual. Similarly, in our speaking and hearing, the possibilities of language—which always is the language of the other used in and constituting social relations—that come to be individualized. This way of approaching language, therefore, turns upon its head the received presupposition that intersubjectivity is built in conversation: intersubjectivity pre-exists the individualization of a specific idea in two or more persons. In this chapter we exemplify how individuals (merely) realize argumentative forms always already existing as collective possibilities.

The Social Nature of the Word

In chapter 2, we quote Vygotsky as having said that the word is impossible for one but a possibility for two. He wrote the paragraphs in which the quotation appears near the end of his life, perhaps in the first part of 1934. It represents his Spinozist period during which he abandoned the intellectualist approach to language and sought to develop an approach that is based on the unity/identity of intellect and affect. Unity/identity hear means that there are not two things but one, which manifests both intellectual and affective qualities. Already five years earlier, Vygotsky wrote a text fragment that was only posthumously published with the title "Concrete Human Psychology" (Vygotsky 1989). In it he suggests that (a) a "word was a command for others," (b) "thinking is speech," that is, a conversation with oneself, and (c) "reflection is a dispute" (p. 57). He writes that in the case of the infant, one can actually follow the development of speech: "First, the word must acquire sense (a relation to things) in itself ... then the child's mother uses it functionally as a word, and, finally, the child does so" (p. 57). However, even before children use or comprehend words, they already use other forms of signs. Indeed, a page before writing what we quote here Vygotsky relates a case exemplifying the birth of a sign in the life of an infant. The particular sign is a pointing gesture.

The pointing gesture emerges from the hand movements of a child. The mother, perceiving the gesture to be in the direction of an object, takes the object and hands it to the infant. That is, the mother treats the movement as an instruction to hand the object to the infant. Eventually, once this has happened a number of times, the child will intentionally point. Actually, Vygotsky describes the initial movement as a failed attempt at grasping the object. However, intentionality is not innate. Intention itself is an outcome of social relations of the kind where an infant's movement that is followed by the movement of another comes to result both in intentionality and in the perception of objects as separate from the self (Mead 1932). Gestures have been shown to emerge already in the non-human animal world. It has been observed among the bonobo in the context of mothers picking up their infants (Hutchins and Johnson 2009). A pick-up requires coordinated movements of mother and infant until the latter is in the arms of the former. Researchers have observed how infants familiar with a pick-up will produce an aspect of their part of the joint movement and then freeze in the position. When the mother, being further away, sees that frozen movement, it will approach the infant and then they perform the pick-up. Here, the pick-up is a collective (social) behavior. But producing part of it outside of the immediate physical relation will initiate a pick-up. That is, the frozen movement has begun to serve as a signifier the function of which (i.e. its signified) might be glossed as, "Mom, come pick me up." The frozen movement has become a signifier because the mother has treated it as such by returning to the infant and picking it up. Here, as Vygotsky (1989) suggests, the sign[ifier] (word) is born when the mother treats (functionally uses) it as such.

In the elementary school, students already are linguistically competent. But they do not yet reason in the way adults do, and especially they do not reason in the way mathematicians and scientists do. In the context of mathematics, it has been shown that mathematical reasoning indeed exists *as* social relation (behavior) first before it is found in the behavior of the individual (Roth 2016). In the following, we investigate the emergence of argumentation in early elementary school. We build on chapter 2, where we describe the individual turn at talk as social rather than as

Fig. 4.1 This artistic rendering of a mixed second- and third-grade classroom shows how the students sit along an approximate arc at one end of which the teacher (right) is situated.

individual. It is social because (a) a word that is sounding in the mouth of the speaker simultaneously is ringing in the ears of the listener (*corresponding*) and (b) the word in the ear of the listener is received, transformed, and evaluated in and with the reply (*responding*).

In this chapter, we draw on classroom discussions that occurred in a multi-age classroom including eight second-grade and eight third-grade students (age approximately 7–8 years). The classroom teacher was dedicated to teaching science and scientific process. She had considerable experience, including several years of previous science teaching in informal settings followed by more than five years teaching science at the elementary school level. During the lessons, she manifested the intent to develop students' scientific thinking and problem-solving skills. For example, she often used phrases such as, "let's be scientists," "scientists can be wrong too," or "I am not saying that's wrong. I am just saying you can think about other answers." In the particular lessons from which we draw here, the students were sitting on the floor in an arc that also involved the teacher sitting on a chair situated at the end of the arc (Fig. 4.1). Although the flow of the classroom talk frequently had the pattern T–S–T–S···, there were also exchanges of the type T–S–S···.

Argumentation and Emergence

In the constructivist approach, any phenomenon is said to be the result of some construction. The metaphor of construction presupposes that there is some goal, some plan, which is to be realized by the construction. Thus, the early Vygotsky draws on the example that Marx and Engels used to distinguish human architect from a bee, which, in its accuracy of building cells, puts to shame many human craftspersons. But the worst human architects have in advance over the bee that they construct the cell in their heads in advance of building them from wax. This analogy, however, is overly intellectualist and works only when the human builder already knows what is to be built. It does not work in the case of the artist who creates something new, thus, a poet in the strong sense. Poets, creators in an extended sense, do not know in advance what they are building and how they do so until after they have come to a language that allows them to describe and rationalize what they have done (Rorty 1989). Learners are poets in this sense, for they do not know from the outside what they will know once everything is said and done. They cannot therefore orient toward that future knowing and construct it, for if they already knew, they would not have to engage in the construction thereof. A better way of approaching what happens in argumentation generally and in the learning of groups and individuals specifically is to think of emergence and evolution. It is characteristic of emergence that the future does not directly follow and thus cannot be predicted from the past, though it inherently develops out of it. Thus, "the emergent when it appears is always found to follow from the past, but before it appears it does not, by definition, follow from the past" (Mead 1932, p. 2). In Mead's social psychology, emergence is social and sociality has the character of an emergent (rather than teleological) evolution.

In the following lesson fragment, one group of children together with the teaching assistant have gathered around a set of desks on one of which there is a glass jar that is filled with water (Fig. 4.2). They observe the carrots floating when they poured salt into a water jar. The teacher has invited them to generate hypotheses about what makes the carrots float. While observing carrots floating, two girls (Neveah and Erin) start talking.

Fragment 4.1

1 E: look our carrots are floating, and I was right… all the salt has to disintegrate.
2 N: keep stirring
3 E: maybe the carrots soak the salt up, and then they float because uh um the stuff that's in the salt, so that makes it float.
4 N: but carrots soak salt, salt goes in the carrots, weigh more

5 E: if the carrots soak the salt in, maybe it goes (.) *puff*, so it makes it fluffier so it rises, because the stuff in the carrots, because with the– with the– there are not a lot of salt in the weight, there are not a lot of weight in the salt, so maybe it is because of the salt and the weight is not in the salt. so there is not lot of salt adds the weight.

The fragment begins with an *observation* statement: the carrot is floating (turn 1). An *explanation* statement follows immediately: the disintegration of the salt allows it to be taken up by the carrot "because the stuff that's in the salt makes it float" (turn 3). The next statement begins with an *oppositive conjunction* "but,"

Fig. 4.2 This artistic rendering shows the children and the teaching assistant gathered around a water jar in which their pieces of carrot float. The children are asked to generate hypotheses about what makes the carrot float in the water to which salt has been added.

followed by *descriptive* statements—the carrots soak up the salt, the salt goes into the carrots—which leads to the *consequence* that the carrots weigh more (turn 4).

Fragment 4.2

3 E: (says) maybe the carrots soak the salt up, and then they float because uh um the stuff that's in the salt, so that makes it float.	
3 N: (hears) maybe the carrots soak the salt up, and then they float because uh um the stuff that's in the salt, so that makes it float.	4 N: (says) but carrots soak salt, salt goes in the carrots, weigh more
	4 E: (hears) but carrots soak salt, salt goes in the carrots, weigh more

In this turn pair, there are two statements and two voices that are logically contradictory. Indeed, following the approach articulated in chapter 2, the contradiction exists not merely between the two students but indeed within the individual responding. This is quite apparent when we add to the transcription the fact that Neveah is actively attending and replying.

The box surrounding the center part of Fragment 4.2 marks that Neveah's reply arises from and with respect to the words while they are received. *Responding* has its origin in the phrase that is coming *from* the other, and leads into the reply that is designed *for* the other. The contradiction exists within the box. It therefore signifies change. After the fact it might be said that the contradiction *caused* the change, but viewed from within the unity/identity of *responding*, analyzing a unit of change results in a contradiction because its parts differ. Such contradictions therefore are qualities of change and growth, because, at the level of the *con*versation, there is now a contradiction in the smallest conversational unit, the transactions of responding or corresponding. We cannot completely attribute the phrase in turn 4 to Neveah, for the words have their origin in the words of the other. The speaker's active orientation takes place during attention to and reception of the words, which also constitutes a form of commentary to which the reply is oriented. New ideas may emerge and develop in the formation of the reply, which contains thought only once it is completely—for, as we quote Vygotsky in chapter 2, speakers themselves do not have access to their thinking and the resultant thought until after speaking has ended. In the course of subsequent turns, the common transactions, the contradiction is an earlier state that will have sought resolution. The conversation continues with statements that describe the salt in the carrots as making this "puff" (perhaps in the way popcorn puffs when heated). Further conjectural statements make the case that the salt does not add much to the weight of the carrot. Again, in the resulting turn pair, which objectively exists for the two speakers (turn 4 | turn 5), there are contradictory statements that come to be confronted, one stating that the absorption of salt increases the weight of the carrot, the other acknowledging the increase in weight but suggesting that this increase is compensated by the puffing up of the carrot.

As the conversation unfolds, ideas evolve and new ideas emerge—that is to say, these have not been constructed but, unknown until the speaking begins, arise from the transformation of one turn at talk into the subsequent turn. Conversely, as new ideas emerge and develop, the conversation unfolds. The relationship between the temporal unfolding of the conversation and the production of statements (their topics *are* ideas) is a mutually constitutive (dialogical) one. Here, "the problem" exists in and off the confrontation of oppositive statements in the simultaneous transactions responding (within individual) and corresponding (between individuals). The conversation unfolds, oppositive pairs of statements emerge and, in the conversational movement toward a resolution, the conversation develops with the birth of statements manifesting new ideas. That is, when we take *corresponding* as the minimum analytic unit (i.e. category), the interplay of contradiction and resolution is the "engine" that moves the conversation ahead and leads to the emergence and evolution of ideas. "Problem" then is another word for the inner contradiction within *responding*, which expresses itself as a logical contradiction; and a resolution would consist in the emergence of *corresponding* units that no longer contain contradictory statements but agreements. But even though there may be agreement, the existence of a statement for two people inherently means a form of double vision that is a mark of consciousness (mind).

In this approach, we do not have to make "sharing" problematic, because saying that there is a problem and saying that it is shared are but two manifestations of the same phenomenon. Because the category contradiction implies a unit of analysis that consists of a transaction, the problem (contradiction) exists at the level of the *con*versation, which, inherently, is shared—or we would not be investigating a conversation at all. In fact, in the approach outlined in chapter 2, the contradiction (problem) exists *in* and *as* the relation: *corresponding* is a (social) relation between two (or more) people and thus is an event involving both. Here, the contradiction is reflected also at the level of the individual. This is so because when Neveah speaks, the words are not only in her mouth and on her lips but these are also "ringing" in the ears of Erin. Thus, if we take Neveah for the moment as the unit, a contradiction exists between "the stuff in the salt makes the carrot float" ringing in her ear and the "but carrots soak salt, weigh more" that is coming from her mouth (Fragment 4.2). In each case, from one line to the next, we observe correspondence encompassing a contradiction unfold into correspondence encompassing a contradiction. We may indeed understand the reply to be a truncated form of a full reply, which also contains the original speech—which is thereby reported (Vološinov 1930). Speakers generally but not always leave out what they are responding to, which in the present case might have taken the form if Neveah had said, "You said that maybe carrots soak the salt up, and that then they float because the stuff that's in the salt makes it float" and then continued, "but carrots soak salt, salt goes in the carrots, weigh more." In this case, the reported speech would be in the form of indirect speech, "You said that…."

To understand the dynamic of the conversation, the emergence of a contradiction (problem) and its conversational resolution, we thus need to consider turn pairs, where the first of the pair attributed to one speaker is taken as a proxy for what is heard by the next. At the same time, what the second speaker says also is taken as an indication for what s/he has heard. In this way, the contradiction, problem, argument, or conflict exist not only between participants (curly brackets, right in fragment) but also within participants (box, Fragment 4.2). From this "it follows that only the unfinalized and inexhaustible 'man in man' can become a man of the idea, whose image is combined with the image of a fully valid idea" (Bakhtin 1984, p. 86). That is, in each statement we actually find two voices, where the speaking not only reflects what might be considered proper to the speaker but also her response to, and thereby uptake of, the speech of the preceding speaker. Conversational development strives towards the resolution of the contradiction, problem, argument, or conflict within the analytic unit (person, pairs of persons)—without any hope that such an endpoint will actually come to be. This is precisely why dialogical relations are inherently developing ideas that are finalized only when the dialogue has ended. Thus, the "idea is by nature dialogic, and monologue is merely the conventional compositional form of its expression, a form that emerged out of the ideological monologism of modern times" (Bakhtin 1984, p. 88). An idea, therefore, is not something subjective and individual, it is not a solipsistic, psychological formation somehow lodged in an individual's head. An idea inherently and irreducibly is interpersonal, intersubjective, a relation between individual concretizations of collective consciousness. This is so even for the most innovative idea, which another person not only recognizes as an idea but also in its innovative nature. For another person do recognize something as an idea, and as an innovative one specifically, the social nature the idea already is prefigured. It is out of the inherent dialogical relation between ideas that we obtain the emergence of the new so that even a single author of a statement (writer, speaker) cannot know in advance what she will have said when her saying has come to an end. Any author is subject to life, the self-development of which "is independent of the author, of his conscious will and tendencies" (Bakhtin 1984, p. 286).

Some readers might want to object stating the fact that ideas develop in the heads of individuals. But from what we show in chapter 2 it is apparent that what Neveah says has its origin in what she hears Erin say, who, in turn, speaks for the benefit of Erin and the other students in the group. The idea, thus, is the relation between what is actively received, how it is transformed in the reception—about which we know little—and what is produced when the reply comes forth. In other words, in the voice that is speaking, there are the remnants of another voice, the one that has been speaking before and that has been taken up as indirect but dropped speech (Vološinov 1930). Any form of responding reports (quotes), directly or indirectly, actually or dropped, the speech of the other (or the current situation in cases where speech just begins).

Laying the Garden Path in Walking

In the famous poem about the traveler at the crossroads where he has to take one of two roads, Robert Frost makes him go down the less traveled one and concludes that it has made all the difference:

> I shall be telling this with a sigh
> Somewhere ages and ages hence:
> Two roads diverged in a wood, and I–
> I took the one less traveled by,
> And that has made all the difference.
>
> (Robert Frost, *The Road not Taken*)

Any experienced teacher really taking into account what children say knows that they cannot anticipate where the classroom talk is taking them and their students. Every future turn is unseen and thus unforeseen and comes with the possibility of surprise. In whichever way the conversation is unfolding, and on whichever untrodden path it is taking its participants, some time "ages and ages hence" they will be able to say that it is that turn "that has made all the difference." In this section we further elaborate on the idea of emergence and show how any one instant in classroom talk may be taken as a teachable moment, which made something salient and worth learning.

Of the many possibilities to respond to the situation, the next statement (i.e. the teacher's) does not take up the question about the salt and carrots. Instead, another statement (i.e. Ellis in Fragment 4.2) provides an opportunity to pick up on the question about heavier and lighter objects that sink or float. The phrase coming from the teacher's mouth says, with rising intonation that allows us to hear a question, whether it [the rock?] was really heav[ier] or whether it was bigger than the other rock. The reply quietly and hesitatingly states that the speaker does not know and adds, "it was a cage." The next teacher statement does not actually take up on what Ellis has said but constitutes a comment on and evaluation of what his statement has done: brought in evidence for what he has thought. The phrase, thereby, is telling not only Ellis but also everyone else listening that what the preceding phrase has done is providing evidence, which is an important dimension of argumentation. The remainder of the statement is drowned out by another one (turn 5) that directly contradicts what the initial statement has proclaimed (turn 1). The contradiction is made apparent in the use of the contrastive conjunction *but*. The next turn begins with the conjunction *because*, which articulates a reason for whatever precedes and linked to it. Here, the reason pertains to the characteristic of little rocks compared to bigger rocks: these are lighter.

Fragment 4.2
  1 E: in duncan ((*nearby city*)) there is a heavy box of metals. and then there is a lighter box around it. and then when it got– and then … and they were in a boat and when you press the button they would get filled up and the heavy ones floated and the lighter one sank.
  2 T: was it really heavy, or was it bigger than the other rock?
  3 E: ((*hesitatingly*)) I don-know um … it was a cage.
  4 T: I like that you're trying to bring in evidence for why you think that
  5 O: but the lighter ones should
  6 T: but I thought (it didn't match?)
  7 O: float and the bigger ones should sink.
  8   (2.3)
  9 N: cause >littler rocks are lighter than great, bigger rocks<.

Again there is an aspect of argumentation instantiated across a pair of turns. Turn 7 states a claim: lighter rocks should float and bigger rocks should sink. This turn is paired with turn 9, which provides a reason for why "littler rocks" should float: because these are lighter than bigger rocks. That is, this form of compound statements in which a claim is made and a reason is provided is born in and *as* the relation of two students, which is salient once we also transcribe the active attending part of the conversation. We emphasize here the point Vygotsky (1989) makes: higher psychological functions, here in the form of an explanation sentence, exists *as* the relation, because the words literally establish (continues) the relation.

66   CHAPTER 4

Fragment 4.3
5,7 O: (says) the lighter ones should
          float and the bigger ones
          should sink.

| 5,7 N: | (hears) the lighter ones should float and the bigger ones should sink. | 9 N: | (says) cause littler rocks are lighter than great, bigger rocks |

In the event, each is acting upon the other so that we observe transactions. The students relate precisely because they co-participate in the unfolding talk. This is the crux of the point Vygotsky makes, but which is infrequently taken up in a body of scholarly literature that tends to emphasize the occurrence of certain "psychological functions" *in* the relation students have with others—not only more advanced teachers and peers but also with any other peer who might be equally or less advanced. It is in this relation that development can occur because the children themselves produce the argumentative pattern "«claim» *because* «reason»." When a child such as Olivia or Neveah, who previously produced part of this pattern in relation with another (see below) subsequently produces such patterns on her own, we would have evidence that participation in the relation has changed the ways in which they contribute to argumentative forms of classroom talk. In the earlier statement, "So it could be *because* the salt is making carrots heavier ... that helps them float," this pattern is already observable in a statement by a single speaker (Ellis).

The other important aspect observable in this fragment is the *formulation* of what has been done. In the same way that we have to be able to speak a language before having something that we can grammaticalize, we need to be participating in or be familiar with argumentation before we can learn its grammar. *Formulating*, a technical word that denotes the practice putting in words what is or has been done, is put to pedagogical use in naming and thereby making stand out what a child has done as something special and, perhaps, as something to be repeated. It is like naming parts of speech when children first encounter grammar during their elementary school years. In argumentation, the role of evidence is critical to strengthen arguments or claims. Evidence is a critical tool to evaluate claims and persuade others. We observe that the children participate in producing these aspects spontaneously because of the possibilities language itself offers. However, producing the statement forms that are fundamental to argumentation is not enough for more knowledgeable participation in argumentation. Culture enters when parents (or teachers) select from among all the actions of children and, in their responses, only take up some. Above we cite Vygotsky's examples of how toddlers and children learn to intentionally point and use words. It is when the adult treats a child's movement or word as an instruction that the latter begins to point or use words intentionally. In the present instance, Ellis has done something that is an important part of what our culture recognizes to be argumentation. It is through the statement in turn 2 (Fragment 4.2) that this aspect comes to stand out and that it subsequently can become an *intentional* aspect in the children's participation.

A final important aspect is the generation of uncertainty. Uncertainty is an important dimension of the development of conversational topics because it offers opportunities for exploring alternative possibilities of establishing just what a statement has said. Even though we do not know what Ellis hears, the subsequent statement in turn 3 has been shaped by what he has heard and, therefore, by what the teacher has stated.

Fragment 4.4

2 T:	(says) was it really heavy or was it bigger than the other rock?		
2 E:	(hears) was it really heavy or was it bigger than the other rock?	3 E:	(says) I don-know ... it was a cage.

We might gloss turn 2 in this way: "It might not be really heavy bigger than the other rock | Was your observation really correct?" The recipient actively orients toward the speech of another, receives what is heretofore unknown, and prepares for the actual reply. What is said thereby reflects not only the speaker's voice but also that of the preceding speaker whose statement has been taken up. In the movement from turn 2 to turn 4, there emerges a certain level of uncertainty, doubt or hesitance toward the evidence stated and it becomes salient and recognized by others. The hesitant reply is not only paired with the teacher's query but also with the collectively produced counter-statement according to which lighter or smaller objects should float. This sequence creates uncertainty about just what it was that the statement proclaims to have seen and thereby weakens the possible contribution of the "evidence" of turn 1 has brought into the conversation. That is, the initial turn pair produces evidence of literally questionable nature. From the perspective of the conversation, a collective phenomenon, the impact of the statement is weaker than it would have been had turn 1 been paired with an endorsement.

Individualizing Collective Claims and Evidence

An important aspect of language development exists in the *individualization of the social*, which, in science education, is the development of scientific language, reasoning, and argumentation. The notion of the individualization of the social is opposite to that which has been developed in constructivist theory since the work of J. Piaget. This latter position holds that children basically are wild and untamed but become fully functional adults in a process of socialization into collective, cultural forms of society. The children construct, in their own heads, a version of the social that is viable and, in so doing, they become socialized. Language, however, always precedes the infant and child. In participating in relation with others, initially parents and other caregivers, the infant and then child individualizes the forms of language that are part of the relations with others. Language is tied into our everyday lives and indistinguishable from knowing our ways around the world. As we become familiar with the world and competent in navigating it, we also become familiar with and competent in navigating the world. Because language is a system, we can talk about things that we have never talked about before, and, thus, express thoughts and ideas that we have never had before. A person, therefore, only realizes what language already has in store; and, as such, anything that can be said already exists at the collective level. In other word, when we talk (or write) it is language that speaks. Through our speech, it is language that is speaking, a language that we have common with our interlocutors. In our speaking and hearing, the possibilities of language come to be individualized. This way of approaching language, therefore, turns a received presupposition on its head, which is that intersubjectivity is built in conversation. In fact, however, intersubjectivity, the ensemble of sense-giving relations with other people, *pre-exists* the individualization of a specific idea in two or more persons. In this section we exemplify how individuals (merely) realize argumentative forms always already existing as collective possibilities.

In the following fragment from the lesson about carrots that float—which includes the teacher, Ellis, and Neveah—a logical contradiction becomes explicit: the salt in the water is absorbed into the carrots, which thereby become heavier. Out of the statement that the current hypothesis has the carrots soaking up salt arises the articulation of what is marked as "different ideas": an observation is described where smaller pebbles move toward the bottom and the larger and heavier pebbles (rocks) move to the top (e.g. as in a river). The statement is offered up as an analogy, where the salt-soaked carrot, having become heavier, is made to float (turn 2). There is then a repetition of the second to last phrase of the preceding turn (turn 3), which, this time, is said with rising intonation that offers it up as question: "So the salt makes carrots heavier?"

Fragment 4.5

  1 T: you do have the hypothesis that carrots are soaking up some of the salt, and,

  2 E: I have different ideas, I saw this in duncan, at a . . . somewhere in duncan, there's, there's some small rocks around the big box, and if you can press a button, there was a bowl and the bowl gets filled up with water, if you press the button, then the, and then the lighter ones went down to the bottom and then the bigger ones and then heavier one went

>   up to the top. <u>so</u> it could be because <u>the salt is making the carrots heavier</u>, so that helps them float.

> 3 T: <u>so the salt makes carrots heavier</u>?

  4 E: ((*softly*)) heavier.

  5 N: that makes it sink.

  6 T: heavier or lighter?

  7 E: heavier.

  8 N: that makes it sink.

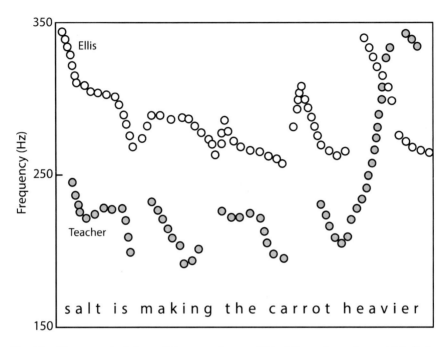

Fig. 4.3 The two articulations of the same phrase exhibit different intonations, which distinguishes the functions of the phrases the conversation. The dictionary sense ("meaning") of the phrases is the same: salt is making the carrot heavier.

Already in chapter 2, we point out the need to investigate why a word or phrase is repeated. Clearly, it is not about the "meaning" of the statement, which is identical in the two cases (see underlined speech in turns 2 and 3). In the common form of transcription above, two speakers say the same phrase, word for word. But in the approach we take in this book, we also need to take into account the active nature of the speaker, which then leads us to recognize that the phrase appears twice from the perspective of the teacher: in her ears and in her mouth, as seen in Fragment 4.3, an extract from the preceding fragment.

Fragment 4.6

2 E:	(says) so … the salt is making the carrots heavier,		
2 T:	(hears) so … the salt is making the carrots heavier.	3 T:	(says) so the salt is making the carrots heavier?

Saying the same words, in the framework we lay out in the preceding section, might at first sight not appear to constitute a contradiction that develops the conversation. But if these words have been repeated, the turn has a conversational and, thereby, developmental function, for otherwise the repetition would be just a repetition. Indeed, even if it were a mere repetition and recognized as such, it would no longer be the same phrase. This is so because the situation has changed, and thus the contexture. The repetition appears as figure against a ground that already includes that same phrase. But not all words have been repeated. From all the words that have been said before, only some appear again in the same order. This makes the five-word phrase stand out against the 77 other words that have been said and heard in the preceding turn. Importantly, the intonation has changed. In the first case (turn 2), the intonation is slightly rising so that the statement can be heard as approaching a continuation, which it indeed does when the implication from the statement follows: "so that helps them float" (Fig. 4.3). It is a factual statement from which something can be concluded: Salt is making the carrots heavier.

In the second case (turn 3), the same words in the same order are said with rising intonation (Fig. 4.3, grey circles). This allows (but does not require) us to hear the phrase as a question. It is not a question about some other state of affair, such as when a person says, "What time is it?" Rather, it is a statement that questions its own veracity. We might gloss the work that the statement is doing in this way: So you are saying "the salt makes carrots heavier"; and I am asking you whether you are sure about that." Speaking softly, Ellis repeats the teacher's last word, "heavier," with falling intonation as is typical for constative phrases, thereby affirming and asserting the semantic content of the statement. Indeed, the phrase does not repeat what would be common sense so that a single word can be heard as a complete statement, which we may gloss in this way: "You are asking me whether salt makes the carrots heavier, and I am affirming, yes it makes the carrots heavier."

In the prosodic movement of the repeated phrase, we also observe that not only does the intonation rise overall, but also the word "heavier" has a much higher pitch, which is hearable as an emphasis (Fig. 4.3). The phrase thus can be heard as questioning the comparative adjective rather than, for example, the salt or water. In the former situation, the phrase might be intonated as, "*salt* is making the carrots heavier?," in which case the emphasis makes "the salt" the psychological subject. In the latter situation, the carrots would be at stake: "salt is making the *carrots* heavier?," in which case "the carrots" would be the psychological subject. The graphic also allows us to see something else typical for conversations in which contrasting ideas can be articulated but in an accepting climate: the teacher phrase begins with a pitch (250 Hz) round about where Ellis ended (270 Hz) before moving into the range more typical of her own (e.g. Roth and Tobin 2010). It is a way of making visible that the questioning occurs in a spirit of solidarity than in one of conflict.

The affirmation of the carrots becoming heavier is paired with an affirmative statement introduced by an implicational "that." Taking into account the hearing part, we may gloss the phrase in this way: If the carrots are heavier, then that makes them sink, as shown in the following fragment, which exhibits the internal logic of this movement from statement to conclusion. Even though Neveah has not stated the implication as a whole, it already exists *for her* in the form of *responding*.

Fragment 4.7

4 E:	(says) [the salt is making the carrots] heavier		
4 N:	(hears) [the salt is making the carrots] heavier	5 N:	(says) that makes it sink.

We observe such compound statements as these appear in the boxed line even when students do not yet use them on their own. But the compound statements exist for them, as seen in Fragment 4.7. That is, it is wrong to state that something is constructed *in* the public sphere of the conversation that Neveah then constructs for herself, in her own mind. In other words, it is wrong to say that she *internalized* something from the public sphere—as we can read this being said and written so many times in reference to the earlier work of Vygotsky.

The inferential statement that emerges in responding therefore constitutes a contradiction to the preceding one, which had stated (in Ellis's mouth and in everyone else's ears) that the carrots float, being made heavier by the salt. The teacher then states "heavier or lighter" with rising intonation, offering up and requesting a statement about the carrots becoming heavier or lighter, as if she had not heard the previous statement (which was indeed almost inaudible) or as if seeking confirmation or as if querying the preceding answer "heavier" itself. Without the next turn, we do not know how and what the individual students hear in the teacher statement query. Ellis's "heavier," articulated with falling intonation so that it can be heard as a constative statement, makes the turn pair a translocution—i.e. *joint* social action—in which confirmation is sought and given. The subsequent translocution constitutes the same inference as that appearing in Fragment 4.6. But this time it stands out more saliently because the phrase could be heard very clearly.

The implication exists not only for Neveah or Ellis, the two speakers, but also for everyone else actively listening. Take the case of Olivia, another student, listening while her peers speak.

Fragment 4.8

4 E:	(says) [the salt is making the carrots] heavier	5 N:	(says) that makes it sink.
4 O:	(hears) [the salt is making the carrots] heavier	5 O:	(hears) that makes it sink.

For Olivia, therefore, there is not something that she needs to internally construct, internalize from the public sphere. Instead, prior to any interpretation or construction she might be engaging in—which, as seen above, is the wrong way of looking at what happens when we hear someone speak—she is actively receiving the phrases and thus the implication. Not only does each part make sense but also the connection between the two. This does not have to mean that she has the capacity to produce such phrases on her own—much like university students do not produce phrases on their own that have any likeness to those that they hear their professors pronounce. But the phrases become one's own once they are taken up in responding, and they have become a person's own when they say phrases that include the complete implication available here in public across the turns 4 and 5.

We note above that even if Neveah had never stated such an inference and even if she had never thought about this phenomenon before, it comes to exist for her in and as the relation, and, therefore, also for her as and, possibly, for everyone else (which we show in the case of Olivia). Language, a system of words and grammar, itself makes the inference possible. It enables the opposite inference in the same way. In both instances (i.e. for Ellis and for Neveah), a collectively possible inference already exists for the individual and thus has been individualized in the sequence of two concrete statements that make a new statement connecting its parts into an implicative whole. Here we do not need to make inferences about what existed (objectively) for the participants. At the level of the conversation, the two inferential statements exist in the form of sound-words that are accessible to every person present in this classroom and actively attending to the unfolding conversation.

In Fragment 4.5, a logical contradiction comes to be articulated between two constative statements concerning the floatability of carrots that become heavier when soaking up salt. The contradiction comes to exist almost despite the individual participants. It comes to exist at the collective level, the conversation; and this is a social through and through because each speech act is in fact a translocution as seen in the various re-transcriptions (Fragments 4.6, 4.7, and 4.8). Every word said, every statement uttered, implies its intelligibility: it is said to make sense. In fact, even a non-intelligible statement can be recognized only against the intelligibility of other statements and, therefore, presupposes mutual intelligibility. The logical contradiction in the content exists at least for us, the analysts and possibly for the teacher. But for this contradiction to have any effect on the unfolding classroom talk itself requires that it be made stand out as figure against ground. Language enables both statements but does not itself provide the criteria whether using one for finding one's way around the world is any more useful than using the other.

This is a place where the teacher has an important function in classroom talk. She can provide resources for making the contradiction salient publicly and, thereby, for influencing the future course of the talk (though she never can determine what actually will occur). Whether this teacher takes up such an agenda and how she does requires further inquiry. At a minimum, this situation creates what educators have come to denote by the term "teachable moment," where an opportunity for teacher moves and student learning arises. How this specifically might happen is articulated in the foundational role societal relations have in learning and development. Thus, just as an inference may be first produced *as* relation (i.e. turn 7 | turn 8), a contradiction may be made salient in turn pairs involving the teacher and students. But the framework articulated here also makes it evident that the teacher has no control over whether the contradiction actually comes to be taken up as the issue in and by the conversation. Because she does not know what students will state in the turns following her own, the conversation may never follow the path she might have intended it to take.

In Fragment 4.2, the statements in turns 3 and 6 have the function of pulling out and making more salient some of the possible topics, here, ascertaining just what is being asserted in the conversation about the relation between the salt added to the water and the carrots. The turns have this function whether the teacher, the teaching aid, or a student articulates it. But we should hope that teachers particularly are in tune with such contradictions. The children make statements, which the teacher takes up and reproduces in part. The conversational development of the topic is produced in the sequentially organized turn-taking sequence and irreducible to the individual. Without the children's contribution, the teacher would have nothing to take up; and without the teacher's contribution, there is nothing for *responding* to be borne on the students' part and some pedagogically interesting developments might not occur. Rather than theorizing this situation as an *inter*action, as many received approaches tend to do, we think about classroom talk globally and each phrase locally as social phenomena that cannot be reduced to the individual participants. The specific teacher and students whom we observe here are but staff of a collective phenomenon, which can be produced involving other staff.

Resolution of Contradictions and Emergence of New Trouble

Argumentation is a dialogical process where different ideas are in confrontation, leading to a continuous unforeseeable evolution towards a resolution of the differences. This confrontation exists both between participants and within participants (in the form of *responding*). Confrontation emerges and then is resolved. It is revoked by a conversational dynamics that no one can predict in its unfolding. The uncertainty and tension around confrontation opens up avenues for new ideas, new claims, and new questions that moves the overall activity ahead. In the fragments shown above, there are instances of confrontation in the conversation around the contention that salt makes carrots float confronted by the idea that salt makes carrots heavier. Although individual students may actually voice the claims with their mouths, these are claims only because they are simultaneously received in the ears of the other who responds. The ensembles of {claim | counter-claim}, therefore, do not belong to individuals. Each {claim | counter-claim} constitutes an irreducible evental unity/identity; it is a movement from one to the other. It therefore also contains an inner contradiction. It is in this form that the movement argumentation has its most basic form. The argumentation is a public event that any participant and onlooker can witness. It is objective in the sense that it can be referred to, even though individual witnesses may (and likely do) differ on precisely what has happened and why. But because each speaker is addressing the other, what is stated implies its intelligibility. Intelligibility thus pre-exists the individual speaker, who already anticipates what makes sense to the other; and this anticipation requires foreknowledge. There is also tension surrounding the narrative evidence concerning the floating of heavier rocks and the sinking of the lighter rocks. This narrative challenges and is challenged by a subsequent statement according to which heavier objects cannot float. In this section we provide an account of how the situation comes to be resolved while revoking the contradiction into another direction. But the resolution itself generates (the possibility) of further contradictions.

In Fragment 4.9, the tension arising from the narrative about the sinking and floating of heavy and light rocks received further like by another narrative pertaining to the same aquarium. The opening statement (Ken) includes a reference to knowing the reasons for the earlier narrative, a fact that the claim attributes to speaker's own experience of having been to the aquarium (turn 1). In this turn, we do see the kind of argumentative structure in a single statement in the way that the teacher formulates as a desirable structure: The statement consists of a claim—"I know why Ellis is saying"—and concludes with the articulation of a reason—"I've been there too." Evidence is provided as the statement unfolds: holding the "big rock" reveals that it was made of plastic. In the exchange that ensues, the conversation brings to the fore that the "big rock" floats while the smaller ones sink when water is added. Again, we observe the "«claim» *because* «reason»" pattern play itself out *across* speakers (i.e. turn 4 | turn 5). That is, this pattern characteristic of argumentation exists here not merely *in* the relation but more importantly *as* the relation between two people. It also exists *for* the relation, as every speaking turn produces talk for the other in response to something that has come from the other.

Fragment 4.9
  1 K: I know why Ellis is saying that bigger one was floating because I've been there too. you could hold the rocks, and the big one was actually plastic.
  2 T: oh, so it looks like a big heavy rock, it's sitting in the middle,
  3 K: yea.
  4 T: and it floats when you add water, and the other things sink to the bottom even though they look smaller,
  5 K: yea, because plastics are actually lighter than actual rocks.
  6 T: but I like how you are using evidence, because you said you saw a heavy rock floating in the water but now we know it wasn't really rock, it was made out of plastic, was tricking us.
  7 E: yap.

The talk provides markers to exhibit that "providing evidence" is desirable. In the highlighting something like an intention, in the same way as the teacher before, which *formulates* that what Ellis has done is providing evidence. That is, not only Ellis but also everyone else has been able to see the practice of "providing evidence" in the immediately preceding exchange. Turn 6 uses the verb "to like" in transitive form, the object being the use of evidence. There is a further elaboration of just what the evidence consists of: seeing the heavy rock floating and knowing that it was not a real rock. That is, in this statement we observe a retrospective denotation as a prior turn to have provided evidence, and a re-articulation of precisely in and as of what the evidence consisted of. The statement further articulates possible problems with evidence of observational nature: observation can be tricked, and this weakens it as evidence. This turn shows that the previously stated observation is not wrong but incomplete with a missing part that was not revealed to the observer (Ellis) at that time. This is another process of *formulating* the importance of using evidence and further the importance of complete and thorough observation as evidence in dialogical argumentation. When observation as a way of data collection is not complete or accurate, it is not strong evidence and cannot support any arguments based on it. The initial observation (Ellis) is completed and becomes evidence *in* and *through* the social relation with another (Ken). By putting the two pieces of information together, the statement makes the important relationship between observation and evidence, and argument salient and public.

In this turn 6, there is a generation of inclusivity. The phrases, "*now we* know" and "tricking *us*," whereby the language designates those present to be part of a larger unit engaged in the process of constituting the intelligibility of natural phenomena. Although the statement may have been unrelated to the framework elaborated here, it is in fact consistent with the observations and explanations that we provide: the *con*versation is an irreducible *social* phenomenon, a translocution, which therefore needs to be treated as a *social* rather than individual fact. The confrontations among the observation, evidence, and claim emerge in relations of the entire group, including children and teacher. The account of the aquarium visit that comes to be articulated is contradictory only when it is confronted with the idea that heavier objects sink. For the evolution of the conversation, it does not actually matter who has physically produced the statement, for it would not have had an effect on the conversation had the statement not simultaneously resonated in the ears of the recipients. The contradiction does work as contradiction only when it operates at the level of the conversation, the dialogical relation, where it belongs speakers and recipients, that is, to the group as a whole. It is precisely because argumentation is a demonstrably public affair, where its different parts—contradiction, evidence, or claims—can be pointed to, formulated, repeated, and explicitly shown in their functioning that children participating in such situations learn to argument. It is not, however, that they somehow internalize what has happened before publicly: their own concrete and public contributions presuppose relevant processes that reflect the outer ones on an internal plane.

In Fragment 4.9, a contradiction is resolved. But the resolution of contradictions does not mean that these disappear. In fact, the theory of emergence suggests that at any point novelty is produced that could not have been anticipated on the past history of a conversation (Mead 1932). Thus, at any point in classroom talk, new contradictions can and often are likely to emerge. This is not a negative aspect of classroom talk but rather constitutes the very generativity that brings forth opportunities for changing participation in changing practices. In the following we show this also to be the case in the present whole-class conversation concerning the floating of carrots when salt is added to water.

The classroom talk around the evidence on the plastic object resolves the tension of uncertainty; but it also brings back the contradiction in the reasons for the floating carrots. The statement that the floating object seen in the museum is plastic suggests that light objects float and heavy ones sink. This confirms the earlier-made claim that heavier things sink. The contradiction within the sequence of phrases "heavier means sink | carrots soaked salt and got heavier | carrots floated" comes into the conversation and leads the whole class once again back to the question, "why did the carrots float?" Another opportunity for making claims arises in Fragment 4.10 (turn 1).

Fragment 4.10
 1 T: do we have another completely different ideas?
 2 K: when Ellis used– just said, maybe the salt is making carrots lighter.
 3 T: so you think the salt is making carrots lighter.
 4 K: yea.

What Ellis is said to have stated about the floating rock had been heard in class. Once a word is said it may be taken up and thus be reported in future speech. In affiliating (turn 4) with the incorrectly reported speech (turn 2), the earlier claim content comes to be contradicted. Instead of carrots getting heavier, they now get lighter by the absorption of salt. We also note how the teacher attributes, in the mundane attitude, attributes what has been said to the thought of Ken, though we do not know what he is thinking at that very instant. The new claim leads another question of how salt makes carrots lighter. The conversation takes a surprising turn in Fragment 4.11 with the suggestion that salt was eating up the carrots (Corby, turn 1). We notice how a claim—turn 1, rephrased in turn 2—is turned into a hypothesis (turn 4).

Fragment 4.11
 1 C: I think the salt is eating the carrots.
 2 T: like dissolving the carrots?
 3 C: yea!
 4 T: a little bit? that's a hypothesis then?
 5 Ss: yes.
 6 T: that the salt dissolves part of carrots?
 7 Ss: yes, yes.

The process of making claims arises out of the unity/identity of thinking and speaking (Vygotsky 1987). The series of claims—salt was soaked into carrots → salt made carrots heavier → salt made carrots lighter → salt dissolved part of carrots—is enabled by the conversation where children and teacher interdependently contribute to the evolving conversation. When something makes sense in the communication of something—e.g. a feeling, belief, or content of consciousness—its content inherently belongs to a class of phenomena and the perspectives of others (Mead 1932). The instants where contradictions appear and become salient are positive and necessary to move forward toward resolution.

The Social Nature of Argumentation

In this book we propose an alternative to common conceptions of argumentation by closely examining children's argumentation. From our analyses emerge descriptions that are consistent with conceptions of language that have their origin in cultural-historical (dialogical) conceptions. Our analytic approach emphasizes that the origin of internal dialogue and higher psychological functions are inherently embedded in societal relations where argumentation takes place (here argumentation in an elementary school science lesson). In this framework, argumentation exists *as* and *for* the relation, which makes it social in a strong sense; that argumentation involves a number of people—i.e. that it exists *in* the relation—only makes for its social character in a weak sense. To understand dialogical process of argumentation, this study investigated how second-/third-grade children participated in science classroom talk and how argumentative discourse emerged and developed in, for, and as relations. Rather than understanding argumentation as a change in individual student talk and writing, we investigated the place where argumentation first appears: in collective and dialogical reasoning processes.

We use fragments from science classroom talk to show how argumentation emerges and exists as transaction and thus as joint social action. Argumentative discourse—such as contradiction and problem situating, claim making and evidence evaluation—emerges and evolves as children actively participated in speaking turns. For example, when Erin and Neveah are talking about their observation on floating carrots, the phenomenon of floating carrots becomes problematic. When Erin states that the salt is soaked into the carrot pieces and makes them float, the reply states, "*but* ... weigh more." A logical contradiction between floating and weight is emerging in the movements that we refer to here as *corresponding* and *responding* (see chapter 2). A problem (contradiction) is not a problem prior to children's speaking turns or prior to their making an issue of the real problem to be talked about. The contradiction is stated, felt, and situated through exchanges that concretize *argumentative* discourse at the collective level even though none of the children may use such argumentative forms on their own. This moment of evolving a problem is critical in argumentation discourse. It situates children in the problem of logically contradictory statements, a crucial basis of argumentation. Another example of argumentation as transaction can be seen in the episode of floating rock. Ellis and Ken are explaining their experiences of a floating rock in water tank. Through the conversational engagement, the weight of carrots becomes a salient problem. Different evidence is given, evaluated, rejected, and accepted throughout the exchanges and a new claim is created to respond to the problematic issue. It is in the different positions, in the different voices, that the problem first comes to exist. Our analysis therefore is ethnographically adequate in the sense that it shows where the argumentation *first* becomes visible: *in, as,* and *for* the relation. Every turn pair is a transaction, simultaneously involving movements in opposing directions. We thus show how argumentative discourse (claim making and evidence evaluating) is collectively processed and developed. Any claim made comes about through a joint evaluation of evidence. The irreducible and inevitable nature of collective argumentation engenders the need of different approach to teaching and understanding children's reasoning and argumentation.

The tension of argumentation exists in problematic situations and it comes into our consciousness only though dialogues. In this chapter we exhibit different levels of tension as these arise in the evolution of argumentation. The emergence of tension and the tension of emergence is a driving force to children and teacher to evolve and develop argumentation. In the lessons, moments of tension emerge and are recognized. Such tensions first exist in turn pairs, such as in the "but … weigh more" and the revision of an earlier statement as "puff." This tension at the level of the conversation situates children in the emerging contradiction. The individuals, such as Erin and Neveah are only staff in a tension that exceeds both of them before their individual statements include such tensions as points of development. There is also tension in evaluating evidence around the floating rock. The *contradiction* between the heavy rock rising or sinking *first* exists as translocution. We may perhaps at some later time find one or the other participant deliberating on his/her own in the way the deliberation here occurs involving several of them. That is, any form of argumentation may arise at the level of the conversation and then may show up when the same individual takes on those previously distributed parts of the argumentation.

References

Bakhtin, M. M. (1984). *Problems of Dostoevsky's poetics*. Austin, TX: University of Texas Press.
Hutchins, E., & Johnson, C. M. (2009). Modeling the emergence of language as an embodied collective activity. *Topics in Cognitive Science, 1*, 523–546.
Mead, G. H. (1932). *Philosophy of the present*. Chicago, IL: University of Chicago Press.
Rorty, R. (1989). *Contingency, irony, and solidarity*. Cambridge: Cambridge University Press.
Roth, W.-M. (2008). The nature of scientific conceptions: A discursive psychological perspective. *Educational Research Review, 3*, 30–50.
Roth, W.-M. (2016). On the social nature of mathematical reasoning. *For the Learning of Mathematics, 36*(2), 34–39.
Roth, W.-M., & Tobin, K. (2010). Solidarity and conflict: Aligned and misaligned prosody as a transactional resource in intra- and intercultural communication involving power differences. *Cultural Studies of Science Education, 5*, 805–847.
Vološinov, V. N. (1930). *Marksizm i filosofija jazyka: osnovnye problemy sociologičeskogo metoda v nauke o jazyke* [Marxism and philosophy of language: Application of the sociological method in linguistics]. Leningrad: Priboj.
Vygotsky, L. S. (1989). Concrete human psychology. *Soviet Psychology, 27*(2), 53–77.

5

The Role of Physical Objects in Science Lessons

Physical objects as tools of thinking and learning mediate children, the teacher, and intended curriculum. In typical scenes of hands-on activities in science classrooms, materials are brought up and introduced for children to explore the materials and develop the understandings of science concepts and skills. The physical objects are taken as only a tool for children as learning agency to achieve the intended learning outcomes. As research in science education focuses much on children's learning and teacher's teaching as pedagogical objects, there has been lack of interests and research in what roles physical objects play in science classrooms. Physical objects are often put into the background of children's learning, which is overlooked, thus, out of study interests. Yet, physical objects often become the anchor of children's reasoning and argumentation with and without teachers' intention. For instance, the mystery object (tulip bulbs) in chapter 2 played a significant role in the emergence and development of children's reasoning and argumentation. The object was complexly intertwined with experiences, observation, discussion and negotiation of knowledge at the scene and further was taken to the object of argumentative discourse in the classroom. The presence of the physical object oriented and led children's thinking, actions, and classroom discourse into certain directions.

Physical objects are also chosen as sources for data, claim making, and evidence evaluation in practical work. Teachers, who have made decisions about intended learning outcomes, generally choose physical objects for accuracy and precision of data collection based on practicality and accessibility of materials. Especially when there is a strong desire on attaining specific science concepts through practical experiments, materials are chosen to generate clear data and patterns and less potential of errors in material operations. Students' conclusion will be drawn from data collected, which attain the science concepts. Argumentation is not expected to happen in this process unless things go wrong (Roberts and Duggan 2007). Some materials are chosen also for critical reasoning and creativity to open questions, wonder, and doubts. In the example of the tulip bulb activity, the object opened space for children and the teacher to wonder, question, doubt, and negotiate ideas and the emergence of argumentation and tension of problem solving were evident throughout the class discussion. Some physical objects, even without teachers' intention, appear to foster the emergence of critical reasoning and argumentation. What is it in the tulip bulbs that encouraged children to articulate many different claims and evidence to convince each other and the teacher? What roles do physical objects play in children's reasoning and argumentation? In this chapter, we bring physical objects to the center of classroom interactions and discussion in order to understand the roles and functions of physical objects in children's reasoning and learning.

The Commonness and Difference of Physical Objects

Children's critical reasoning in knowledge negotiation and argumentation could develop where there are different and contradictory claims shared to explain phenomena. For instance, when children observe falling snow and make claims such as (a) "the snow is white" and (b) "it melts on my hands," there may be no contradiction in their claims as both are observed and accepted, thus no argumentation emerges. Yet, when children make such claims, a contradiction might be articulated in the communicative exchange because children do not agree. The contradiction inherently presupposes that the object exists for all, though their perspectives *inherently* differ (e.g. Mead 1938). We may then think of multiple parties to a situation and their relation in terms of the analogy with eyes: two eyes do not just lead to a composite picture, they lead to a new type of picture, one in three dimensions. That is, multiple perspectives provide a totally new phenomenon: the social, that is, that which is inherently shared (thus intersubjective). Together, the multiple perspectives give "a binocular view in depth. This double view *is* the relationship" (Bateson 1979, p. 133). Thus, when the snow is turning into rain-like sleets, the conversation might take on a new dimension when the event of precipitation is introduced. The physical object, the cold stuff falling from the sky is present and tangible to be observed and experienced at the very moment and invites children's thoughts, words, and interactions. The object was felt, described, and shared in the public. The difference between snow and rain is immanent in the very physical object and further provide potential of argumentation discourse. That is, the nature of sleet already has the immanence of argumentation discourse in its physical property to the question of what it is.

In science classrooms, teachers often introduce various hands-on materials for curriculum purposes. How do children interact with classroom materials? How do materials unfold a space of thinking and reasoning? Are there any physical objects that embody the immanence of argumentation more than others? The following episode examines how physical objects emerge and are developed as questions and contradictions during hands-on activities.

Table 5.1 *Examples of children's claims and evidence on their science notebooks*

	Noel (Grade 3)	Ken (Grade 2)
Marble	Sink because it is glass and glass sinks.	Sink because I atchaly (actually) thrown.
Ping-pong ball	float because it is light.	Float because I loset my ping-pong ball
White soap	sink because I have dropped soap in the bath.	Float because I did it in the bath
Orange soap	sink because the same as above.	The same as that
Wooden artefact	float because I have seen a tree that is in the water.	It dapands wate (depends what) kind of wood it is.
Pearl necklace	sink because it is heavy.	Float because it will flot
Lego blocks	float because they have seen it float in the bathtub.	Float I atchaly did it

Children and the teacher in a second- and third-grade science classroom were engaged in exploring the concept of floatability and buoyancy. Various materials, including marbles, ping-pong balls, two bars of soap (almost in the same size but different colors; white and orange), a wooden artefact, pearl necklace and Lego blocks were introduced in the beginning of the class. Those materials can be found in everyday life, where children often already have had experiences with them. These preceding experiences are then articulated in the public forum of the whole-class exchange. The teacher asked children to predict if they would sink or float and explain reasons for their predictions. Children in small groups observed each material and wrote down their predictions and explanations on their individual science notebooks. The materials were touched, weighed by hands, and reflected by everyday experiences for children's explanation. In other words, the materials provided moments of palpable and imaginary understanding of floatability. Table 5.1 presents some examples of children's predictions and reasons. Although Noel and Ken wrote these statements in their science notebooks, these are not just their own. These statements are intended for another—including the teacher and peers—and, thus, incorporate the view of these others (cf. Mead 1938).

Children reflected on their everyday experiences and heaviness of the materials to explain their prediction. Some claims are based on everyday experiences, e.g. they saw things float or sink and some are based on their ideas on heaviness, e.g. it would float because it is light. In children's prediction, the marble is an object that sinks and the ping-pong ball and Lego blocks float. Different claims were made concerning the soaps, wooden artifact, and pearl necklace. The same or different claims are made with respect to children's science notebooks as physical objects exist in different perceptions, experiences and contacts of children. Up to this point, the objects simply and harmoniously existed in the complex situation including object, medium, and organism. But the characteristics of those objects perceived and described were challenged by the question of the floatability of the objects. Now, these physical objects became sources of contradictions because of the different experiences, claims and evidence in the classroom and the floatability of the physical objects needed to be conducted and understood in public through solving.

Next class, the teacher and children sat on the carpet and reviewed their predictions and reasons from the previous class before testing the materials in water. When the teacher asked what they predicted on the marble, children said, "sink!" and on ping-pong ball, they said, "float!" She asked them to speak out if there were any different ideas when they went through the list of materials. There were no disagreements expressed in public on marble (sink), ping-pong ball (float), wooden artefact (float), pearl necklace (sink), and Lego block (float). An agreement on those materials was reached without many speech turns. For example, concerning the wooden artifact, children shared their experiences with observing tree parts floating on the river or lake to support the claim, "it will float." This was agreed and accepted shortly without further discussion. Ken who wrote down, "it depends on what kind of wood it is," and subsequently did not make any further comments on this during the class discussion (Table 5.1). However, when discussion touched the question whether the soap bars would float or sink, the conversation did not produce an agreement, as different claims and reasons for them were produced. The conversation produced many statements about the two soaps, as apparent in Fragment 5.1.

Fragment 5.1

  1 T: did you think both of them were the same? how about the orange soap? did you think float or sink?
  2 Ss: sink!
  3 T: did you think it would sink. okay. why did you think it's gonna sink? do you have evidence for your claim?
  4 O: because it's heavy.
  5 N: because when you drop a bar of soap in the bath, it sinks to the bottom.
  6 O: if you have bubbles in the bath, and you dropped the soap, then you have to go like this ((*she is acting as if trying to look for the soap by touching the bottom of the bathtub*)) to find it.
  7 N: you can't just get it out. you have to get all the way down to get it out.
  8 T: so you've had a bath and seen the soap sink to the bottom. so that's good evidence.
  9 K: yea, but sometimes different kinds of soap float and sink.
10 T: so you think different kinds of soap may act differently?
11 K: yes. ((*Noel shakes her head.*))
….
12 O: actually I kind of think the white soap might float.
13 T: so you think the white soap might float and the orange soap might sink? jason?
14 J: um, both will float.

The claims about the soaps are conflicting in this dialogue. When the claim, "the soaps will sink" was stated, it was supported with the evidence of children's experiences such as "when I dropped a soap in the bath, it sank to the bottom." While the claim was being shared and supported by some children through verbal support and silent nodding, another claim, "different kinds of soap float and sink" was also publically shared. In one instance (turn 9), the statement "so you've had a bath and seen the soap sink to the bottom. so that's good evidence" is taken up and modified in the return, soap bars "yah, but sometimes different kinds of soap float and sink." This claim opens possibilities of new claims that the two soaps could act differently, that is, one might sink and the other might float. Noel voices disagreement by shaking her head when the teacher questions if children think different kinds of soap may act differently. Now, several claims are made and shared in public.

– Claim 1: Soaps will sink because they have seen soap sinking to the bottom of the bathtub.
– Claim 2: Sometimes different kinds of soap float and sink.
– Claim 3: One (white or orange) may sink and the other may float.
– Claim 4: Both will float.

The soap bars led to many statements, some of which contradicted each other based on different observations and different claims in the exchange. Not like other objects which children reached an agreement without conflicts, several competing claims concerning the soaps emerged and challenged children's reasoning through several speech turns. What led children's claim-making over the marble and ping-pong balls into an agreement and one over the soaps into conflicts? What part of the soaps affected children's claim making with contradiction? To explain why they think soaps will sink, children's everyday experiences in the bathtub were reflected and articulated: "when you drop a soap in the bathtub, you have to look for the soap in the bottom of it." This evidence was supported by several children in class who might have experienced it in their homes. The soap in their experiences and knowledge is to sink. The commonness of soaps was built around their experiences of soaps in the bathtub and shared in the making of claim-evidence. Then, a new claim, "soaps can also float" emerged and challenged the consensus related to the floatability of soaps.

The nature of physical objects is already and always social as they exist, are experienced, and understood in and through social relations. The commonness of the floatability of soaps was already embedded in the material itself, as they are in children's play and experiences in everyday lives. The soaps commonly seen and experienced in the bathtub sank but children also observed some soaps floating, such as when Ken wrote in his science notebook that it would "float because I did it in the bath" (Table 5.1). The deviation (floating soaps) from the commonness (sinking soaps) was shared, challenging children to engage each other over their claims. Through this social interaction, the commonness and deviation in buoyancy and floatability became to co-exist in the white and orange soaps to be argued and negotiated. Unlike marbles and ping-pong balls suggested the commonness of prior experience—i.e. marbles always sink and ping-pong balls always float—soaps provided a complex context for children's claim-evidence making.

In human experience and knowledge of physical objects, there exist the preconditions of the objects, which invite, orient, and develop human actions and reflection on the objects (Mead 1938). In the constructivist approach, these objects exist subjectively for humans; in social constructivism, these different perspectives are then negotiated, shared, and culturally handed on. However, for social psychologists with a cultural-historical bend (e.g. Mead 1938), objects *inherently* are social objects. A physical object existing for one person alone is impossible, but it is a possibility for two (Feuerbach 1946). In the same way, a word is impossible for one person but a possibility for two (Vygotsky 1987). The floatability and density of certain physical objects as preconditions presuppose human experiences of throwing them in the water. Thus, the precondition of physical objects provides a for the commonness of sense-giving contexts in and through human experiences. For instance, the physical material glass has certain characteristics to be glass. It shows, acts, and feels like glass differently from metal, wood, or plastics. It is used for certain purposes such as windows, bowls, cups, etc., not for chairs or clothes. The commonness of glass is experienced, learned, and shared in children's experiences and knowledge of it, which orient their thinking, reasoning and problem solving. When children need to choose a material for building windows, they would agree to choose glass rather than plastic or wood. The transparency of glass, the commonness as precondition presupposes the need of glass for the window. The *ideal* of glass is immanent in the object itself to orient children's collective decision making.

The commonness of physical objects can be challenged by deviations in materials or problem solving contexts in classrooms. For example, if glass that is provided to children is opaque, this manipulation of material choice could challenge children's decision making. The material, opaque glass challenges the ideal of glass in transparency and thus the commonness of the sense-giving contexture for decision making as it will not be good for windows to look out. This develops the possibilities of negotiation and argumentation. In other words, physical objects already have something in common to be challenged with differences, which orients and develops children's thinking and talking into argumentative discourse. In fact, deviations themselves *are* forms of relations emerging in and from relations. Depending on the availability, diversity, and manipulation of materials, children's reasoning emerges and expands when their activity is taken into new and different directions. The processes of claim-making, evidence-seeking, and evaluating actions, no longer attributable to the children alone, is a function of and arising from the physical presence and actions of materials.

Abstraction: What is Happening in the Real Event?

The deviation from "the ideal soap that sinks" requires further investigation among children. The teacher brought a basin of water and children started to drop the objects into the water. Most of the materials behaved in the way that the children predicted. The marble sinks, the ping-pong ball floats, the wooden artefact floats, the pearl necklace sinks, and the Lego block floats. They record their observation in their notebooks. Then, the two soaps do not match their predictions. The white soap floats and orange soap sinks. The children call the teacher and say, "Ms. Kelly, Ms. Kelly, the white soap floats!" Now the two soaps in action act differently from the ideal soaps that sink in the bathtub. Soaps can float or sink as the white soap floats and the orange soap sinks. The commonness of soaps is no longer common or ideal in their observation on the floating soap. The presence of two soaps in the water, one on the bottom and the other on the surface challenges the claim that "the two soaps will sink because when you drop a bar of soap in the bath, it sinks to the bottom." The different actions of soap bars lead to statements of surprise (Fragment 5.2a).

The children are back on the carpet when the teacher opens a class discussion. The teacher asks if there were any surprises in their observation.

Fragment 5.2a
1 T: were there any surprises? talk to me about your observations. any surprises?
2 E: I thought the white soap would sink but it floated.
3 T: the white soap floated and the
4 E: the orange soap sank!

The event was a surprise. To see something as a surprise, it occurs other than what common sense anticipates. The common sense that a soap bar sinks is now challenged and disproved by the floating white soap. Then a new question emerges through the teacher's action. The teacher holds up the two soaps and moves the orange soap down to present the physical objects in the event (Fragment 5.2b). The white soap stays afloat but the orange soap bar starts sinking. Why?

Physical objects are considered concrete and real, that is expected to provide children opportunities to learn abstract concepts in science classrooms. The abstract concept, buoyancy and floatability could be sensed, concretized, and understood through observation and manipulation of physical materials. The two soap bars in two different locations in the water provided the opportunity for an observation categorical: "different soaps act differently." The observation categorical pertains to multiple observations simultaneously (Quine 1995), here to the floatability of soap bars rather than of a single soap bar. The observation categorical leads children's reasoning to focus on why one floats and the other sinks (turn 1, Fragment 5.2b).

Fragment 5.2b

1 T: so I have a question for you. does anybody have any guesses, any claims why this floated and this sank?

2 N: maybe there were different molecules in them, maybe the orange soap, the molecules aren't buoyant, and so they sank and other soap, they are buoyant.
3 T: so what you are saying that they are made of different materials?
4 N: yes.
5 T: okay, cate, you have any ideas why one sank and one floated?
6 C: the smell has, the molecules have the smell that make not buoyant so it sank
7 T: so you think they added scent to this and so maybe a bit more dense cause they added scent.
8 C: yes.
9 T: okay, that's an interesting idea as well.
10 K: that's probably because the white soap doesn't have anything on it but the orange soap, it's because ((*he stands up and gets close to the teacher, grabs the soap*)), if you have it, this one is solid but this one, you can see through it.
11 T: okay, this one you can see light through it, and this one you can't.
12 K: and that, maybe also because the wrap was coming off a lot, maybe some of the water is getting into the wrap, going under it, going in the place where it wasn't open and putting more pressure on the bottom of it.

As the physical objects in the event provided evidence for the counter claim, different soaps act differently, the classroom discussion was developing to explain why they see the claim in action. Why did these two soaps act differently? Why did the orange soap not act like an ideal soap in the bathtub? The teacher questions *why this floated and this sank*, taking the orange soap down (turn 1). The physical objects representing the event are at the center of classroom problem solving. The differences in properties were discussed; some molecules in the orange soaps were not buoyant (turn 2), the molecules that have the smell make not buoyant (turn 6), things that made the orange soap see through made it sink (turn 10), and the air pocket filled with water made it sink (turn 12). The difference between the two soaps was available to children and the teacher to observe and was explained in public. Whatever made the two soaps different in texture, scents, transparence, and wrapping made them act differently. The floatability and buoyancy of soaps were observed and abstracted in the event and now explained and shared among children as follows.

– The two soaps have different types of molecules, one is buoyant and the other is not.
– The scent added to the orange soap made it sink.

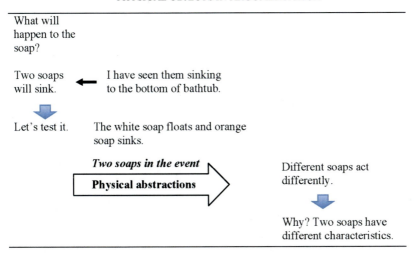

Fig. 5.1 *Physical abstraction in the event*

– Something translucent in the orange soap made it sink.
– The water getting inside the wrap made the orange soap sink.

The overview of problem solving on soap floatability is shown in Fig. 5.1. Starting from the question, "what will happen to the soap," claim and counter claim making, testing and data collection, and sense making of the results took place and, the soaps in the event became the center of reasoning. The differences were existent and accessible in the physical entities to trigger children's reasoning. The soaps became the joint tool in their talking, thinking and understanding the event of sinking and floating objects, i.e. abstraction of floatability and buoyancy.

Physical Objects that Contribute to the Making of Sense

In the episode above (Fragment 5.2b), physical objects exist at the center of children's learning and knowing of floatability. Children and the teacher think, talk, and reason with the physical objects. The physical materials thus also support the exchanges in a strong sense. This is so because the relation of the participants—e.g. in the words exchanged—determines their relation to the physical world, and the relation of humans to the physical world determines the relation between them (Marx and Engels 1978). The concreteness of materialistic presence provides ways of abstracting the materials in the context of floatability and the abstraction of physical events is only possible through material interactions. The soaps were bonding the teacher and children's touching, viewing, talking, and reasoning to think about why one floated and the other sank (Fragment 5.3). This moment of when the phenomenon begins to make sense emerges around physical interactions with the soaps for children to negotiate and revise their claim-evidence relationships.

In these speech turns, physical objects open and complete the sense-giving contextures for floatability. The physical performance, the objects and language are inseparable in this meaning-making moment. In these turns, the white soap and orange soap are replaced with the words, "it" (Fragment 5.3, turn 10, offprint a) and "this one" (turn 10, offprint b and turn 11, offprint c), which does not explain much without the actual grab of the objects. Children's reasoning and explanation are inseparable from the physical objects and their own performances. The evidence and claim for floatability only make sense when the physical objects are present and interacted at the scene.

Fragment 5.3 (excerpt from Fragment 5.2b)

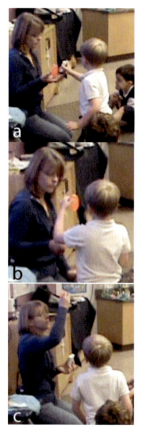

10 K (says): That's probably because the white soap doesn't have anything on it but the orange soap, it's because, if you have *it* (a), *this one* is solid but *this one*, you can see through it (b).

    (Others hear and see) That's probably because the white soap doesn't have anything on it but the orange soap, it's because, if you have *it* [white soap] (a), *this one* [white soap] is solid but *this one* [orange soap], you can see through *it* [orange soap] (b).

11 (Others hear and see) Ok, *this one* [orange soap] you can see light through it [orange soap], not like window, actually could see his face, but definitely see light through *it* [orange soap], but *this one* [white soap] you can't (c).

    T (says): Ok, *this one* you can see light through *it*, not like window, actually could see his face, but definitely see light through *it*, but *this one* you can't (c).

In the excerpt above, the physical objects are fundamental to process the dialogue, thinking, and problem solving. Without the physical presence, the conversation does not make sense to each other. In part this is so because the objects are available to their physical senses, most importantly here the sense of vision. Whatever differences there might exist, the presence of something is itself not questioned. The sentence, "if you have *it, this one* is solid but *this one*, you can see through *it"* (turn 10) does not mean much in terms of children's reasoning and explanation. Only with the enacts of physical objects, others hear, "if you have *the white soap, this white soap* is solid, but *the orange soap*, you can see through *the orange soap*" and understand the attempt of making sense of floatability through the different texture of the two soaps. The objects are becoming inseparable part of perception, language, actions, and reasoning process at the scene. The physical objects contribute to the sense making process. They complete the words, the sentence and the meaning of what's being said at the scene, thus, it is an essential tool for children's reasoning and dialogue to understand science concepts.

Learning with Physical Objects

Physical objects function as a tool to provide differences and contradictions for children's reasoning and classroom talk. The episode of two soaps shows how the presence and event of physical materials anchored and organized children's claim making and reasoning. Children's talk and action emerged and evolved along with the unfolding presence and event of physical objects. As physical objects are experienced together in classrooms, they embody the preconditions of human experience and knowledge, i.e. the co-existence of commonality and deviation. The marbles, ping-pong balls, and soaps that already exist in children's previous experiences are now revealed in a new light in the context of the question whether they float or sink. In this context, the commonness of certain objects emerges; marbles sink, ping-pong balls float, and soaps sink in the bathtub. Unlike marbles and ping-pong balls, the common sense concerning soaps that sink in the bathtub was challenged with the possibility of floating as claim. When there was a deviation and difference from the commonness emerged as new data in the events of the two soaps, children's thinking, reasoning, and talk were challenged and developed into new questions, new claims, and new ideas. Compared to other materials in this episode, the two soaps presupposed difference as surprises in the objects. The commonness of rocks in floatability is that rocks always sink and they sank in real events. The common sense related to a ping-pong ball is that it floats; and here it floated on the water as expected. There was less opportunity of difference and deviation from the common sense. Yet the possibility of deviation and difference was immanent in the soaps. The different and surprising event as new evidence anchored and oriented children's thinking, talk and action in the activity.

As physical objects are shared and experienced collectively, the difference and contradictions are also possible, which emerge and then lead to the development of children's reasoning and argumentative discourse in classrooms. Physical objects exist as mutual foci in communicative exchanges, and thus contribute to bonding and contributing to classroom exchanges. An example of this can be seen in the Fragments 5.2b and 5.3, where the physical objects were the center of classroom talk and collective reasoning. In the sociology of emotion, mutual focus is a central concept (Collins 2004). In joint activities where there is something at stake, mutual focus leads to the mutual entrainment of affect, attention, and cognitive experience. The concept of entrainment was borrowed from physics, where it refers to the fact that two clocks of different period change these periods until they are in synchrony when mounted sufficiently close on a common background. Our previous research in second-grade mathematics classroom has shown that common focus and resonance phenomena, which also are observed in the conceptual dimensions of an event, are fundamental to learning the practices of a discipline, including mathematics in a second-grade classroom (Roth 2011). Our studies of argumentation in elementary classrooms show that with seeing, pointing at, and touching the two soaps, children and the teacher were making sense of the floating and sinking soaps. Without pointing at the soaps as speaker and seeing them as receiver, the words and sentences do not make sense in the exchange. The physical objects exist for two (or more) participants and are inseparable from the classroom exchanges and reasoning processes. In this case, it is critical to understand how physical objects are perceived, interacted, and immersed in collective talk to understand how children's reasoning processes and develops.

A physical object in science classrooms is no longer a simple entity for hands-on manipulation for learning science concepts. It contributes to organizing and giving shape to the lesson, curriculum and children's learning, focusing the verbal exchanges on something that is material, concrete, and existing for everyone rather than something like a concept, which does not inherently exist for everyone in the same way that a unicorn or ghost does not exist for everyone.

References

Bateson, G. (1979). *Mind and nature: A necessary unity*. New York, NY: E. P. Dutton.
Collins, R. (2004). *Interaction ritual chains*. Princeton, NJ: Princeton University Press.
Feuerbach, L. (1846). *Sämtliche Werke. Zweiter Band. Philosophische Kritiken und Grundsätze* [Complete works, Vol. 2. Philosophical critiques and principles]. Leipzig: Otto Wigand.
Gott, R., & Duggan, S. (2007). A framework for practical work in science and scientific literacy through argumentation. *Research in Science & Technological Education, 25*(3), 271–291.
Marx, K., & Engels, F. (1978). *Werke band 3* [Works Vol. 3]. Berlin: Dietz.
Mead, G. H. (1938). *Philosophy of the act*. Chicago, IL: University of Chicago Press.
Quine, W. V. (1995). *From stimulus to science*. Cambridge, MA: Harvard University Press.
Rorty, R. (1989). *Solidarity, contingency, irony*. Cambridge: Cambridge University Press.
Roth, W.-M. (2011). *Geometry as objective science in elementary classrooms: Mathematics in the flesh*. New York, NY: Routledge.
Vygotsky, L. S. (1987). *The collected works of L. S. Vygotsky: Problems of general psychology* (Vol. 1). New York, NY: Springer.

6

Argumentation and Inscriptions

Anyone opening a scientific research article or a science textbook will see the abundance of items other than verbal statements. These items include graphs, tables, lists, photographs, diagrams, spreadsheets, and equations. In classical psychological research, such things are classified as *representations* because they present something again (re-). For example, a photograph presents, and thus makes present again the person depicted. But we can also try to imagine in our private minds how the person looked. Classical psychological research also calls a representation such a making present in the mind, a type of imagining. The term representation thus is confusing because it refers both to something that is private and non-material—there is no actual physical image like a photograph in our minds—and to something that is public and material. In anthropological and sociological studies, where researchers tend to refrain from speculating about the mental contents of people, the term *inscription* has become the common way of referring to graphs, tables, lists, photographs, diagrams, spreadsheets, and equations (Roth and McGinn 1998). The concept itself makes clear that it classifies things that are somewhere *inscribed*, either on a piece of paper, in an electronic document, on a chalkboard (whiteboard), or in any other suitable medium (e.g. wood or stone, or drawings in the sand).

In the classical take on inscriptions, such as those that appear in scientific research articles, a direct correspondence is assumed to exist between the structure of a natural phenomenon and mathematical structure, often expressed in graphical form. More recent studies, especially those with social constructivist referents, point to the arbitrary ("socially constructed") nature of the relation between the structures of the natural world and those in mathematical (graphical) form. When the relationship is iconic—when a specific multi-pulley (system) is modeled with a generic, one-pulley system—then this characterization of the relation as arbitrary is more difficult to see. Yet in many ethnographic studies of scientific research work, the ontological difference between a phenomenon and any graphical depiction is accepted. The difference exists even if scientists were to take a piece of soil every 20 centimeters from a longer column in a soil corer and place these in a series of boxes (Latour 1993). The stratification of the soil in the natural world still would differ from this series, even though it consists of concrete soil. The scientists may argue over a drawer with an array of the soil samples collected, representing extension and depth of the soil in a particular area, and point to the different locations of the array as they speak. (One dimension of the array in the drawer represents the location of the collection site along a line and the other represents the depth from which the sample was taken.) But it would indeed be impossible to make a scientific argument in the discipline using the soil-filled drawer as evidence. Instead, the scientists will resort to making diagrams in their articles and reports that show the extent and depth of the different soil components that they found Whatever they use, the actual soil samples or diagrams, will serve as evidence in support of some claim.

The purpose of this chapter is to describe and theorize the role of inscriptions in argumentation, with a particular attention to the opportunities that inscriptions offer to argumentation in the elementary science classroom.

A Lesson Fragment

In this chapter, we draw on a lesson fragment from the mixed sixth- and seventh-grade science classroom that also features in chapter 2. The teacher had challenged the students to a tug of war. Initially he had invited eight students. Then, as the teacher pulled the students toward the line where winning and losing was decided, more and more students joined. Even a student in a wheelchair joined. To increase the resistance, he also put the breaks on. In the end, 20 students, which amounted to almost the entire class, were pulling: with now avail. The students lost. Once all the students were sitting again, the teacher, in saying "what happened here?," initiated what turned out to be a 15-minute exchange about why the students lost and how the block and tackle needed to be set up so that the teacher would not be advantaged. An integral part of the lesson were the diagrams used to model the actual tug of war and alternative set ups that would not be to the advantage of the teacher. Initially the teacher made some of these drawings, but, when it became apparent that there was confusion about the locations where the system was to be attached or where the different parties were to pull, the teacher invited students to the chalkboard. When everything was said and done, the chalkboard was littered with diagrams (Fig. 6.1) some of which had taken the place of others that were wiped off in the course of the talk.

Viewing the lesson on video, we notice that the first five minutes of the whole-class discussion establishes an explanation of why the teacher has won the tug-of-war even though there were more than 20 students on the other end. Then, in what after the fact is recognized to have been a major shift, students propose alternative designs. In the end, seven designs are considered, three of which clearly are seen when the discussion comes to a close (Fig. 6.1). The teacher has drawn the first

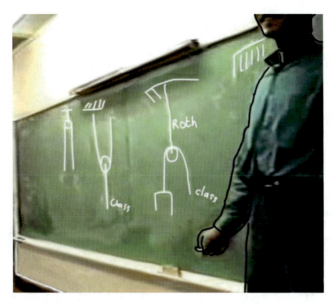

Fig. 6.1 At the end of the whole-class discussion, the chalkboard was littered with drawings that the teacher or students drew while talking the design of a pulley system to be used in a tug of war. Some drawings were erased and their place taken by others.

two, and, following students' instructions, has added to more. Students draw the three remaining diagrams in the course of their talk.

Shamir gets particularly involved, repeatedly taking the speaking floor. For example, early on in the discussion, he argues: "You were pulling your own string, though, like one end of the string was tied to tha tha end thing, and you were just pulling it, and the pulley was attached to the thing, so when you pull, the whole pulley moves and everyone on the string moves with you." He also suggests that the class was holding up the teacher, so that if students had led go of the rope, the teacher "would be off somewhere." Later he suggest that if the class had pulled really hard, it would have torn the banister—to which the block and tackle was attached—out of the ground. Still later, he adds that the teacher would have been in a city some 400 kilometers away; this comment earns him a lot of laughter from other students. Across his several contributions, he made two claims: (a) the banister was holding the teacher up; and (b) the class was holding the teacher up.

Eventually, Shamir says in orienting himself to the teacher: "you can have the banister" and "you can have the banister on your side." In saying "Does anyone understand what Shamir is asking me?" also marks the student's comments as something difficult to understand, which is confirmed when several other students call out "No!" He even says, "I still can't imagine what you are trying to say." Shamir offers to come to the chalkboard, but the offer is not taken up. Eventually, the teacher selects Don to come up and draw the situation that Shamir is describing, but, after an initial attempt, Don selects Shamir, and, when the latter arrives near the board, reaches him the piece of chalk. In chapter 2, we already analyze the

94   CHAPTER 6

first few seconds of the performance, which takes place over the diagram that Don has left behind. After the end of the earlier fragment (Fig. 2.4), and even though the teacher holds the student accountable for the already existing banister on the board, Shamir wipes off what he had drawn in replacement of Don's diagram and begins anew.

Fragment 6.1
```
 1 S:   <banister>
 2 ?:   uh hm
 3 T:   okay,
 4 S:   <long string>
 5 T:   okay, (0.1) pulley
 6 S:   ⎡<roth>  ⎤
 7 ?:   ⎣hh. KHh⎦
 8      (0.8)
 9 S:   pull here. ((hand movement along rope))
10      (1.2)
11 S:   ⎡ok ay⎤
12 T:   ⎣ok ay⎦
13      (0.3)
14 S:   an'then there is a pulley
15      (0.6)
16 T:   >an'where=d'you< (.) pull.
```

```
17 ?:   hn hn hn
18      (1.2)
19 S:   and there is another <banister>
20 ?s:  ha hn hhn ha ((laughter))
21      (0.5)
22 S:   <and we pull> (0.7) here. ((writes "class,"
        see Fig. 6.1))
23 ?s:  ((clap 8 times))
24 ?:   yeAAA
25 S:   you, ye j'st–
26 D:   AH:::::A.
27 T:   okay, thank you very much, (0.4) can you–
        ((hand movement inviting Shamir to sit))
28      (0.6)
29 ?    but AH::
30 A:   but then mister (.) doctor roth doesn't have
        anything to pull at.
31 T:   ((claps six times)).
32 S:   that's just, that's my point
33 ?s   (2.9) ((many students are talking at the same time))
34 S:   now let's try it and then you'll be hugely beat.
```

The point of his performance is to provide evidence for an earlier claim: There is a way of setting up the tug of war where the teacher could have the banister on his side but the class would win. That claim is summarily stated at the end of Fragment 6.1: "Now let's try [this configuration] and you will be *hugely* beat" (turn 34). In the course of the fragment Shamir provides the evidence for his case: the teacher can have the banister on his side and still loses. The prosodic variation, and the step-by-step construction of the diagram, makes for a dramatic performance. Repeatedly, some of his classmates laugh or clap their hands.

In the end, and even though there is a lot of laughter and applause for the case Shamir makes in the course of the lesson fragment, one of his classmates (Aslam) voices a critique (turn 30), which can be glossed in this way: If the tug of war takes place in the configuration as Shamir has just completed drawing, then the teacher does not have to pull at all. Here, it is the teacher's turn to clap six times. But Shamir still says that this *is* his point. Over the next 2.9 seconds, many students apparently talk about the performance, though it is impossible to hear what any one says in particular. The videotape does allow us to hear the apparent summary of the case Shamir has made: the evidence he has provided is such that in a new trial at the tug of war, the teacher will be hugely beat. The discussion ends here, as the teacher initiates another task. What Shamir says is not clear, and we do not know at all what he might have said if the discussion had gone on. Because of what we write in chapter 2 about the relation between thinking, thought, and speech, it would be complete speculation to ascertain anything about the ideas he might have had. Whatever a researcher might claim about Shamir's conception would be completely off the mark. We also do not know what might have been in the teacher's head, or his motivation. Accepting the precepts that a concrete human psychology only deals with whatever is available in the public sphere to all participants, we take seriously the need to provide incontrovertible evidence that is available to any actual or vicarious participants of the debate.

In this fragment specifically and in the entirety of his contributions more generally, there is an event that has Shamir taking the orientation of an opponent to the teacher. The orientation actually has two sides. On the one hand, the event has him take that side in the argumentation that is opposite to the teacher's. On the other hand, the case they are debating is an actual tug of war and its hypothetical alternative in which Shamir and the teacher are on opposite sides of the game. The drawings are an integral part of the case that the event has Shamir make; and it is the role or relation of these drawings to the argumentation as a whole that we are concerned with in the section "Inscriptions in Argumentation." Before getting there, however, we focus on the changes in classroom talk and what the talk accomplishes.

96 CHAPTER 6

From Explaining an Observation to Warranting a Claim

We note above that the entire discussion concerning the tug of war can be divided into two phases. First, initiated by the invitation to comment on what has happened in the tug of war, the talk concerns finding an explanation. In his curriculum related notes, the teacher is concerned with allowing students to talk pulleys, and, in so doing, develop competencies in pulley-related discourse. That early part of the classroom talk is a search for an explanation. Here, the tug of war constitutes the data, the outcome is given ("students lost"), and the talk concerns the warrant, why did the students lose or, alternatively, why did the teacher win? This structure may be depicted diagrammatically (Fig. 6.2a). The warrants initially are given verbally, but the talk itself is treated as ambiguous, as seen in the fact that the teacher, while seeking to ascertain what a student has said, begins drawing a pulley configuration.

Fragment 6.2
 1 D: uh hm you were pulling the pulley and I think that gave you the advantage over eight or nine of us or ten, and you were winning till Ian's wheel stopped and then you had an advantage over us.
 2 S: uh um (2.0) you were pulling your own string, though, like one end of the string was tied to tha– tha end thing, and you were just pulling it, and the pulley was attached to the thing, so when you pull, the whole pulley moves and everyone on the string moves with you.
 3 T: so you are saying that one pulley is attached, one side attached? ((*begins drawing a pulley configuration*))

From the outset, it is not apparent whether the drawings based on the first and second descriptions would be the same or different. But, because there are alternative competing explanations (warrants) offered for the outcome, each turn is a claim for an appropriate warrant. This is the situation presented in Fig. 6.2a. An example of the request for a secondary warrant occurs in Fragment 6.3, in which the query–reply pair requests and provides a warrant for his claim that the teacher has been in the position B during the tug of war here represented diagrammatically. Readers may also note the qualifier "you think," which is the second person form of "I think" that speakers include in a statement and thereby weaken its strength. Statements that include an attribution to a specific person have been categorized as the weakest form; they are on the first of five levels, where the highest level corresponds to the statement of uncontested facts (Latour and Woolgar 1979). On the other hand, the statement that the class has lost is uncontested. Everybody present has seen that the teacher won the tug of war in pulling more than 20 students across the line. That the class had lost is treated as an incontrovertible, objective fact. Other things were more flexible and open to be contested.

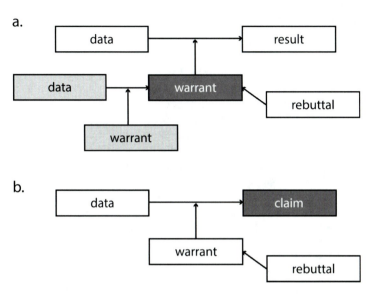

Fig. 6.2 **a** The early part of the classroom talk about the tug of war sought an explanation for the result of the competition. The different explanations (warrants) are contested, requiring data and warrants. **b** In the second part of the talk, the claim "we would have won" is discussed, and different warrants are produced—and themselves contested (rebutted).

Fragment 6.3
 1 D: you were on B.
 2 T: Don, why do you think I was on B?
> 3 D: because you were pulling on the little rope attached to the pulley, and we were just going in a circle.

In this tug-of-war-related talk warrants are not simply accepted but here and there are contested in turn. For example, the warrant that the teacher was supported comes to be paired with a question about the nature of the support (turn 2, Fragment 6.4), which finds its reply in "the pulley." The pulley, which is to warrant the claim about the nature of the support to the teacher, becomes the target of a contestation in a turn that states the opposite: the pulley supported the students ("us," turn 5).

Fragment 6.4
 1 D: supports, strong supports.
 2 T: who supported me?
 3 M: the pulley.

4 T: okay, the pulley
5 AJ: us–, that supported us.

In this classroom talk, finding an explanation is not the only concern. Here and there, statements are made concerning an alternative outcome, as in "You would have lost if there was a thousand people" (Aslam) or "if we had let go you would have been in Kelowna" (Don, Shamir). This concern is associated while considering specific configurations, which are discarded because they are found not to be viable. For example, in the statement "if the other rope is hold onto there, then we wouldn't be pulling anything," a cause and effect relation is made; it is then supported by the warrant "cause it's stuck onto there" (Chantelle). After about 7 minutes, there is an articulation of what might be heard as a summary and an offer to conclude the discussion: "I [teacher] had an advantage, I had a mechanical advantage, and Daniel used another word last period, which was to *gear down*, (.) what I did, we geared down all of your effort, so that I actually could hold it." The events show, however, that this will not have been the summary of the talk because a claim is offered up that the class would be winning even if the teacher had the banister on his side under the condition that "the pulley there, if that was on our side" (Shamir). Now the in-order-to motive of the talk is to provide a warrant for a claim (Fig. 6.2b), which takes the form "the class would be winning." It is out of this new situation that the talk transcribed in Fragment 6.1 arises. After the warrant is presented, a rebuttal comes from the students. In the configuration offered (i.e. the warrant), the teacher "doesn't have anything to pull at" (turn 30 in Fragment 6.1). In the following section, we exhibit the function of inscriptions in the establishment of a warrant.

Inscriptions in the Establishment of a Warrant

In the preceding sections, we present the unfolding of a lesson sequence in which the outcome of an earlier tug of war becomes the content of classroom talk. Notably, the talk about the tug of war does not take place over and about the material configuration itself, involving a block and tackle consisting of two sets of conjoined pulleys, a tangle of ropes, and a banister to which one rope is attached. The actual set up is complex and not easily comprehended even if drawn to scale. However, the pulleys can be represented such that the actual configuration that the teacher set up during the recess becomes intelligible (Fig. 6.3). The diagram shows that the block and tackle used during the tug of war was equivalent to an arrangement of five pulleys combined into two groups of joined pulleys. Readers immediately note that what appears on the chalkboard is unlike the diagram depicting the actual set up—where there are multiple pulleys combined into two sets as opposed to the single pulleys that the teacher and students draw during the discussion. Yet in an abstract form, the pulleys, rope, banister(s), and competitors are all there. All the diagrams that appear are inscriptions that abstract from the actual situation

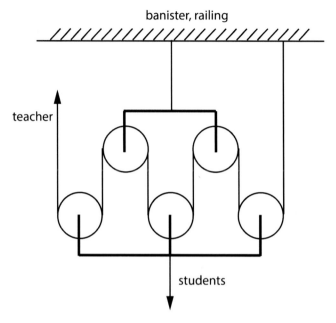

Fig. 6.3 The setup of the tug of war using a separation of pulleys. There are two sets of pulleys. One set is attached to the railing (banister), whereas students pull on the other one. A third rope is attaché on one end to the banister, flows through the pulleys, and is pulled on by the teacher on the other end. The result is a five to one reduction of the student-supplied force.

depicting it as a type with which they are familiar. Prior to that lesson, students already have seen and measured the relationships between the forces acting in systems that only involve one pulley, including the two configurations that can be seen on the left side of the chalkboard (Fig. 6.1). The relative simplicity of the design allows it to be grasped perceptually so that it may be used as a warrant for explaining the actual outcome of the tug of war or making claims about hypothetical tug of wars that students would win. It is apparent that the actual mechanical advantage is not important at that time in the face of navigating the conceptual issues involved. In this, the inscription obtains a simplicity that is reminiscent of the diagrams that the physicist R. Feynman introduced to make visible the interactions and relations of fundamental particles in collisions. Feynman's pictorial representations reduce the complexity of the mathematical expressions that they stand for and that would be difficult to grasp intuitively. Just as theoretical physicists were enabled in face-to-face meetings to support their argumentation concerning particular processes in high-energy collisions by means of Feynman diagrams, the diagrams appearing the chalkboard enabled the participants in talking conceptual issues in the design of a tug of war without getting caught up in the details of the actual setup.

Even more important than the omitted step of replacing the depiction of the configuration of the tug of war with the block and tackle to the simple diagram is the movement from the actual thing, the tangle of ropes and block and tackle to the inscription. The step is an ontological one, from one cluster of matter with a particular form (here: ropes, block and tackle, banister, people) to another cluster of matter with a particular form (here: chalk lines on chalkboard, words) (Latour 1993). The abstraction from the actual materials comes with a gain: universality. Whatever pulley or block and tackle involved, and however many pulleys there are in each of the two blocks, the argument holds.

Using inscriptions rather than words also comes with affordances for the discussions that words or equations do not have. In the chain of ontologically distinct representations that links the real world, on one end, and language, on the other hand, mathematical equations, graphs, and language are more abstract than the diagrams that at least preserve some perceptual similarity with the phenomenon. This facilitates the classroom talk, where there were apparent difficulties when participants attempted to express themselves using words only, made apparent in Fragment 6.5.

Fragment 6.5

1 S: if we were B but you had the banister on your side like if the banister was on that side– okay, just say there was a banister on that side.
2 T: does anyone understand what Shamir is asking me?
3 ?s: NO
4 D: I do.
5 T: Devin?
6 D: what if there is a railing over there and we were B and, and you still had the railing?
7 T: I still can't imagine what you– what you are trying to say.

Here, even though the diagram is present, the content of the talk is marked as difficult to understand and as difficult to envision while speakers are not near the thing (here inscription) being talked *about*. In themselves, the words fail to communicate. This failure may to a large extent arise from the fact that there are many words generally classified in linguistics as *indexical terms*, including "there," "that," and "over there." A term is indexical when it is pointing to something relative to the speaker. The expression "that side" orients to a side away from the speaker, whereas the expression "this side" makes salient the side closer to the speaker. These indexical terms have their equivalent expressions in pointing gestures, where an imaginary line through the stretched-out finger reaches a place or object that is distant or near. As we show in chapter 2, however, a finger configuration is pointing only when there is something pointed at, and something is pointed at only when there is a pointing finger (or other body configuration). Similarly, the words "here" and "there" make sense only when there already is a situational configuration that motivates the use of these terms; and the particular configuration of places near and distant becomes salient in the use of these words.

The same may be said about other words as well. Take for instance the term "banister." It is indexical in the same way as the terms "here," "there," and "that."

This is so because there already is something that shows itself—here the horizontal line above which crosshatches are found (Fragment 6.5)—that motivates the use of the word. Conversely, the very use of the words makes the line with crosshatches salient, accents the banister (railing) thing and renders it visible by allowing it to become figure against ground.

The events show that the talk remains non-intelligible—even though the talk occurs in the presence of the diagrams on the chalkboard. The talk is *about* the diagram, which stands in for the complex real-world tug of war involving a block and tackle. Something changes when Shamir comes to the front of the classroom and close to the chalkboard. Now, in addition to the words in the presence of the diagram, drawing and hand movements *over* the diagram are enabled to support the evolution of a warrant in support of the claim, "the class would be winning all the while the teacher can have the banister on his side." The performance that follows reduces ambiguities that were present in earlier warrants. First, drawing a line functions in the same way as pointing to the line—but may be much less ambiguous. In chapter 2, we describe how an action makes sense in a contexture of actions (including non-actions, not doing something). Here, a line becomes visible and salient by the very fact that it is drawn. Unless a pointing gesture comes so close to the thing pointed to that it nearly touches, there remains ambiguity as to what the pointing refers to. Drawing a line is more similar to actually touching it during a pointing movement. The pointing gesture also leaves ambiguity with respect to the thing, because it may refer to the thing as a whole or only to some part. This is quite clear in verbal deixis, where the use of "that" or "over there" in itself may be ambiguous with respect to the nature of the thing or place.

The salience of the line is enhanced with the articulation of the word "banister" (turn 1, Fragment 6.1). There are now two forms of actions both pointing to the crosshatch-enhanced line, and the crosshatch-enhanced line motivates both. In the performance, every part of the pulley system thus comes to be made salient and distinct from other parts each coming with its own name: another banister, a pulley, a rope attributed to the teacher (Roth), a rope end attributed to the class.

There is still more happening. This more is enabled by Shamir's proximity to the inscription. The event has Shamir not only pointing to some rope and saying something "you pull here," but, and more importantly, has the hand move along the specific rope where the pulling is to happen (Fig. 2.4, turn 9 in Fragment 6.1). Now there are hand movements that make visible the actions and the directions in which they are to take place: pulling. In chapter 2, the movement of the hand was from the pulley toward the banister, the actual configuration that occurred during the tug of war. In Fragment 6.1, however, the gesture movement coinciding with the naming of the action is toward the pulley—thus potentially creating another ambiguity. But the direction in which the class would be pulling makes sense again, for there is a clear movement on the rope toward its end and away from the pulley (system).

The final diagram now is available for inspection, critique, and, thus, to a(n) (implicit) rebuttal. Indeed, open for inspection is what the event as a whole, together with the diagram, has presented. Whereas many students earlier replied in the negative when the query about comprehension of the talk is offered, the warrant for the hypothetical tug of war now is intelligible and thus subject to critique and (implied) rebuttal. We do not know how the teacher, in the privacy of his inner consciousness, evaluates the warrant. But the video shows him grinning when Shamir comes to the end of his performance; and the teacher claps his hand in a way that allows seeing it as applause when Aslam states that the teacher does not have to pull at all in the offered configuration for to stand his ground.

These materials show how a pulley lesson moves from an actual tug of war involving a pulley configuration to a whole-class discussion that first is concerned with explaining the outcome and then moves to create alternative configurations for the purpose of warranting the claim that the class could win. Whereas much of the work on argumentation concerns itself with warrants in verbal form, the present materials make visible the integral role that inscriptions may have in the constitution of a warrant. The warrant does not exist in verbal phrases and it does not exist in the combination of verbal phrases and words. The presentation as a whole constitutes a warrant, words, drawing, pointing, and diagram as a whole. The presentation is a unit that cannot be further decomposed because of the mutually constitutive nature of diagram, movements, and talk. It cannot be decomposed because it consists of the entire movement from beginning to the end. It would no longer be that movement if some intermediate stations were accepted, which, in the limit, would consist of something resembling the different photographs on a movie reel. Thus, the presentation cannot be separated from the phenomenon that it is all about: the tug of war and its configuration. The relation between the performance and the actual or potential tug of war is constitutive in the same way as are the relations between (a) the word banister and the crosshatch-enhanced line, (b) the pointing gesture and the crosshatch-enhanced line, or (c) the hand movement along a line and the verb pulling.

In itself, the presentation is not a warrant. Its sense as a warrant depends on the activity as a whole, and the current in-order-to motive specifically. This motive is substantiating a claim about an alternate outcome of the tug of war. That is, the situated performance in itself does not have a sense ("meaning"). It is only in the nested levels of contextures described in chapter 2 that the performance makes sense. In the performance, there are indications of changes in the levels of sense-giving contextures that we need to consider. For example, there are clearly visible changes in orientation. The students orient toward, gaze at, or gesture with respect to the diagrams; but they also orient toward the teacher, who not only was the opponent in the tug of war but also becomes the opponent in the debate. The entire Fragment 6.1, for example, exhibits an oppositional intention: making a convincing case for the claim that the offered pulley configuration was a winning one for students. In this endeavor, the students take an orientation: beating the teacher in a hypothetical tug of war. In and with the performance, Shamir takes up an orientation in a double sense: (a) to the inscription and the hypothetical tug of war and toward (b) the teacher, his opponent in the argument and in the competition. In the process, Shamir moves from evolving the battlefield in a diagrammatic way, and then, turning toward the teacher, animates the configuration with his entire body. The implications this has for how we theorize thinking are worked out in chapter 7.

Until now we are concerned with grasping the sense of the performance with respect to the outcomes of an actual and a hypothetical tug of war. The framework implicit in the preceding analyses is presented in chapter 2. However, this framework does not really suffice so that we need to expand the number of levels investigated to make sense of the event. The tug of war and the related discussion that ensued takes place within a science lesson that is part of schooling. Formal schooling in turn is but one of the many activities that in their ensemble constitute society.

Opportunities Arising from Working on the Chalkboard

Warrants performed over and about the inscriptions on the chalkboard made visible the relationship between the elements (pulley, support, ropes). Our analyses show that what is visible and figure at any point in time does not depend on the words alone; in fact, at times there were very few words. We thus need to expand the Vygotskian idea of language as a sense-giving field that is different from the visible field. We point out the mutually constitutive nature of some visible feature and word or any other form of sign; words, gestures, and other body movements are themselves perceivable events that are co-present with other phenomena (events). Moreover, intonation also needs to be considered; and it is a completely physical phenomenon that makes visible structure in the speech parts that is associated with the psychological (as distinct from the grammatical) subject of a phrase. It is in the performances as a whole that anything "conceptual" is embedded, not in the different things that make up a diagram or a phrase.

In the preceding analyses, we observe that drawings themselves are phenomena similar to language where conceptual issues are expressed in the relationship between words, not in the words themselves. For the present conversation to work at all, relationships between individual parts of the drawings—we may denote them as graphemes—and the physical devices have to be specified. In the early part of the talk, before the discussion as such emerged, a considerable amount of transactional work was to be done to assure that the relationship between (a) the ropes, banister, and block and tackle and (b) the single pulley on the chalkboard made sense. Once the correspondence between device and a first diagram was established, new diagrams also made sense even though they no longer pertained to an actual thing. But in the performances, the link between the inscription and the (present or future) actual device continuously was made explicit. Referring to lines in the diagrams, participants used expressions that also could have been used had the talk occurred over the actual device. These expressions include "you can pull on here ... and then we pull here" (Shamir pointing to the diagram), "but then Mister, Doctor Roth doesn't have anything to pull at" (Aslam pointing to a diagram), and "you guys were pulling on this one here" (the teacher pointing to a rope on the floor). Talk over and about physical devices becomes indistinguishable from talk over and about drawings that represent them.

In a book entitled "What Means Thinking?" (Heidegger 1954), the author points out that thinking should be thought of as a type of handwork, a trade. We learn to think by doing thinking not by acquiring some discourse *about* thinking; and thinking always begins with and emerges out of other events located in the environment and ends, through action, by affecting this environment. Thinking thus is not reducible to the person but has to be thought in terms of the unity/identity of person and environment (Il'enkov 1977), an idea that we develop further in chapter 7. The same can be said about the practice of argumentation, which also involves thinking (see chapter 7). We may denote the process at the lesson at the heart of this chapter by the old English verb *to argument*. We then may describe what students engage in as "doing {argumenting}" generally and as "doing {warranting}" specifically. In the observed practices—patterned actions recognizable and subject to being made visible—the front of the classroom including the chalkboard was a common space in which warranting took place. The performances, together with the space, constitute an evolving situational contexture any part of which could be made salient and become accented visible. The performances themselves are perceptible, and it is only in the mutually constitutive relation that parts of the performances bring to the fore parts of the visible to make it figure. When a lack of comprehension was made apparent, participants could work on constituting the situation so that the performance (words, gesture, pulley configuration) made sense again. In the proximity of the chalkboard, words and gestures that were not intelligible before now came to make sense. Thus, in situations such as those described here, the chalkboard became a medium for the evolution of intelligible and therefore shared warrants—various designs constituted by the different arrangements of the graphemes (various versions of the three basic building blocks, "banister," "pulley," or "string (rope)." In the context of the diagrams, the warrants also took the form of images, which were brought in motion by the physical performances. Diagrams manifested relationships that the performances brought into correspondence with the physical phenomenon. Over the course of the classroom talk, topics were constituted in unitary performances that included verbal, visual, and performative aspects. In a way, these complex performances constituted the warrants as such.

In this situation, therefore, access to the chalkboard enabled intelligible warrants that consisted of more than simply the integration of talking, drawing, and writing. In the speakers' movements, the inscriptions came to live. With sweeping motions of the hand, a speaker animated a diagram and indicated not only the existence of a force but equally important, acted out its direction. In such animation of diagrams, warrants exhibited their full nature as communicative hybrids, which make sense because of the redundancies built into them by the co-occurrence of things that constitute the sense-giving field. In the hand movements, the diagrams retained the dynamic character of the earlier tug-of-war.

A line of research in science education concerns multi-modal practices. The present chapter shows that we must not approach argumentation starting with the different modes to accede to the multi-modal ensemble. Instead, any pair of modes includes mutually constitutive modes—word and line, gesture and line, or word and gesture. These are all constitutive parts of a unitary whole that manifests itself in different, sometimes contradictory ways. Any communicative problems in the constitution of warrants were remediated when speakers used the chalkboard as part of their performance.

The chalkboard was the setting for constructing alternate tug-of-war designs and simultaneously served as a recording device that allowed references between various designs. These diagrams became available in subsequent talk and summary. The drawings became records during and at the end of the lesson. Whereas spoken words are ephemeral and quickly forgotten in the temporal succession of other talk, the diagrams had a certain permanence that was ended only when they were wiped off to make place for the next inscription. The diagrams therefore afforded inspection, analysis, and re-analysis at later points—such as when the event had Aslam pointing out that the teacher did not have to pull at all in the configuration that Shamir had drawn and that was objectively available to everyone present. The diagrams thereby become "fixed points" in the constitution of the warrants. As such, they were inspectable and arguable (i.e. subject to rebuttal).

When talk occurs over and about inscriptions accessible to all participants, conversations may be democratized in the sense of enabling the participation of those who are less eloquent. This therefore enables the inclusion of students in argumentation who otherwise might be less inclined to volunteer speaking. This is so because the orientation of group discussions around a visual display enables the use of expressive modes other than words. As a result, visual displays enable increased participation from those whose presentations include a lot gesture and corporeal performance. The materials from the pulley lesson show that when speakers have free access to the chalkboard there exist an enormous amount of other expressive forms in the production of warrants that are intelligible, make sense, and thus can become the object of inspection, agreement, or rebuttal.

References

Heidegger, M. (1954). *Was heisst Denken* [What is called thinking]. Tübingen: Max Niemeyer.
Il'enkov, E. (1977). *Dialectical logic: Essays in its history and theory*. Moscow: Progress.
Latour, B. (1993). *La clef de Berlin et autres leçons d'un amateur de sciences* [The key to Berlin and other lessons of a science lover]. Paris: La Découverte.
Roth, W.-M., & McGinn, M. K. (1998). Inscriptions: Toward a theory of representing as social practice. *Review of Educational Research, 68*, 35–59.

7

Argumentation and the Thinking Body

One of the enduring questions that psychologists as much as philosophers wrestle with is: How can the mind, something non-physical (metaphysical) bring about a movement of the body? How can the mind-brain generate the sound-words that we and others articulate? The reader may quickly jump to the conclusion that the process is something like the computer, which converts any text into sound, or which processes information and then renders it auditorily. But, the computer does not have consciousness. The computer does not know that it does something. The question is how something that appears in consciousness, the plan to do or say something, comes to lead to words in our mouths or actions of our feet, hands, or other body parts. That question cannot be solved beginning with the body—physiology, computer hardware—or with the mind (consciousness). Vygotsky was very explicit about the need to begin with the unity/identity of thinking and speech, which, to him, was the royal road toward this core problem of all of psychology. All considerations of how to think about the unity/identity of speaking and thinking, body and thought, tend to lead back to the Dutch philosopher B. Spinoza. He begins the theory by postulating a unitary *substance*. This substance manifests itself as body or thought. But, Spinoza points out, by beginning our analyses with body or thought we neither get to grasp the substance nor do we get to the respective complement—from thought we do not get to the body, and from the body we do not get to thought.

In the preceding chapter, we observe the elementary student Shamir while making producing a warrant for the claim that the students could win the tug of war. The warrant consisted in the description of an appropriate configuration of a pulley system that would do just that. In presenting the warrant, Shamir did not use words to mean something that is not there. Indeed, he did not just talk but also draw and write. Moreover, his whole body was part of the exchange, producing both gestures and orienting toward the configuration on the board or the teacher. In the course of the performance, evidence in support of a claim is produced. Clearly expressed here was a concern for winning, both the argument and the tug of war. Argumentation exists in the situation as a whole and thus cannot be reduced to the words alone. Even the words, drawing, and gestures together do not constitute the whole event. Instead, what is expressed makes sense because of the event as a whole. This whole continuously evolves, and, therefore, so does the sense-giving contexture within which any particular sign (word, line, configuration, prosody, or gesture) makes sense. From the background developed in chapter 2, it is apparent that we must not reduce Fragment 6.1 to the contents of Shamir's mind, his (mis-) conceptions, or his prior constructions. Moreover, any thinking was stimulated from the outside, accompanies the presentation, and has an effect on the outside. But whatever happened in the brain itself—producing any inner and outer speech or consciousness—is inaccessible. As we quote Vygotsky in chapter 2, thought does not pre-exist but becomes what it is only in ad through the event of speaking. That is, the thought is available only with speech and more precisely when it speaking has ended. Because so much occurs in the form of bodily movement, it is in fact better to theorize and think about the event in terms of the thinking body. But, as we suggest in this chapter, this body is not material with some computer added on. There is not body plus mind. Instead, pursuing the line of thought that Vygotsky began, we have to seek recourse in the writings of Spinoza. For Vygotsky, the Cartesian body–mind dichotomy—to which he referred as the *psychophysical problem*—could be overcome only by "bringing Spinozism to life in Marxist psychology" (Vygotsky 2010, p. 23). The psychologist was not given the time to develop this approach. However, a Russian philosopher later would read Spinoza through the lens of Marxism, or perhaps Marxism through the lens of Spinozism: In *Dialectical Logic,* E. V. Il'enkov (1977) articulates what later has been recognized as a position on the thinking body that constitutes a philosophical foundation for the theoretical position that Vygotsky was working toward. It is this line of work that we pursue in this chapter.

The science education research literature tends to separate (oppose) body and mind-brain, the individual and the social—even when, such as in the concept of embodiment, strive to overcome the dichotomy but, as shown in philosophical and psychological studies, the very notions of embodiment and enacted (Piagetian) schemata only reproduce dualism in the parallelism of body and mind. The very notion of "embodiment of knowledge" assumes that there are phenomena—mind, curriculum—that are enhanced when embodied and that embodiment makes the relation between formal discourse and contexts. Near the end of his life, Vygotsky turned to the works of the Dutch philosopher B. Spinoza, an opponent of Descartes. This turn to *Spinozism* enabled Vygotsky to make an important step "to a more consistent pursuit of the idea of the *fundamental* identity of the two allegedly polar ... forms of human life the biological and the cultural" (Mikhailov 2001, p. 16). That distinction between the biological body and the cultural mind also maps onto the distinction between the isolated individual and the social collective. Although in the 1930s Vygotsky articulated his critique of the body–mind dualism in standard psychology and although others later offered a viable alternative in what we refer to as the *thinking body*, little has changed in the research community since then. Constructivism, focusing on the mental, is a main obstacle to understanding the relationship between body and mind.

Discursive approaches tend to focus on science students' and teachers' words, expressions (externalizations) of mind or individual subjectivity, independent of the materiality of knowing and learning science. Distinctions are often made between the individual and the social, such as when studies define subjectivity in terms of the egocentric attributes of the individual or when the social relation is merely a context rather than the psychological function itself. One of the ways in which this distinction manifests itself is when researchers write about *internalization*, which is opposite to the position taken by the later Vygotsky in recognizing the unity/identity of the self (person) and other-than-self (environment). The separation of the individual and the social also manifests itself in the research on scientific conceptions and conceptual change, which are attributed to and characteristic of individuals even though, admittedly, some have already argued on discursive psychological grounds, that science conception talk is inherently social and cultural. The later Vygotsky argued strongly against mentalism, for example, in the context of emotions. Such mentalism can be seen when investigators ask their students or teachers to keep emotion journals or to talk about their emotions during interviews. What is written in such journals are not the emotions; it is talk *about* emotions. Mentalism also manifests itself when science educators assess knowing using interviews or written tests, where everything a person knows (or learns) is reduced to words. It is observable even in studies that claim to use a cultural-historical activity theoretic framework and method and use interview data, so that the whole activity is reduced to the phrases articulated in the interview. Cartesianism is present even in those works that declare allegiance to Vygotsky, theorize learning in terms of individual cognition supported by and occurring in social contexts. The psychologist was critiquing not only those forms of psychology that were oriented toward biology, attempting to reduce the problems of the psyche to physiology, but, important in the present context, he was equally critical of "interpretative psychology oriented toward idealistic philosophy" (Vygotsky 1997b, p. 10). In interpretive psychology, as in constructivism, the mind is primary; even the affects (emotions) in the classroom are researched using interviews and thus by means of language, which is the related to everything mental (i.e. to individual or social construction). As a result, "descriptive psychology is *really* developing into fiction" (Vygotsky 1997a, p. 336).

Position and Disposition

In this chapter, we return to the case study of argumentation in an elementary school over and about a tug of war. In chapter 6 we see how a warrant in the form of a diagram featuring the design of the tug of war including a pulley—which is standing in for a block and tackle—emerges as a student–teacher relation. In the performance, the student Shamir clearly takes a position as opponent in the tug of war and as opponent in the argumentation. The double orientation is apparent when Shamir orients toward the chalkboard where he draws the diagram, and the repeated change to an orientation in which the student comes to stand face to face with the teacher, as if in a confrontation (Fig. 7.1). That latter orientation may include the diagram, such as when the student's body is oriented toward the teacher and the hand points toward the place in the tug of war where the teacher would be pulling (Fig. 7.1d). These different orientations are associated with different narrative spaces: (a) one oriented toward and concerned with a two-dimensional inscription and related gestures and (b) the other oriented toward the audience with gestures and movements that take into account the three-dimensional space we live in (Roth and Lawless 2002). In those bodily orientations manifest themselves different in-order-to motives within which the student takes position and has disposition. In the former orientation is exhibited the disposition Shamir is taking toward the warrant that will be the result once everything has been said and done. This orientation is nested in an encompassing one toward the ongoing event of argumentation.

Being positioned comes with particular dispositions to act, which are the result of previous life. Even if Shamir's behavior would not manifest scientific argumentation in the form of the Toulmin argumentation pattern, he would indeed be familiar with taking a stance on something and providing reasons for doing this or that. Providing reasons for behaviors—those of others and our own—is the basis out of which the scientific argumentation pattern arises. The dispositions themselves—here supporting a claim—do not have to be, and in most cases are not, apparent in consciousness: we simply respond to the contingencies of the situation at hand in, and we do so in appropriate ways. Even less are all the things that we do in the process. Thus, when we take up a piece of chalk to make a line or circle on the chalkboard, as Shamir has done, we do not consciously direct our arms, hands, and fingers. There is no exact, slavishly followed plan required to draw a line—in the same way that we do not have all our phrases planned out in our heads before saying them. There is but some vague sense of where we are heading in making the argument—the in-order-to motive—and everything falls in place as we act in a situationally contingent manner to concretize and develop what exists in only a nuclear state.

Being positioned also manifests itself in the voice of speakers, especially in the relation between the pitch and pitch ranges of speakers that follow one another. Previous research shows that speakers who are in agreement with each other and between whom there exists a sense of solidarity, the next speaker tends to begin at a pitch level where the preceding speaker has ended (Roth and Tobin 2010). When people take contradictory position—e.g. have an argument in the mundane sense of the expression—then the pitch levels are not aligned. These observations reported from science classrooms reflect those that have been observed between interviewers and politicians or between children in a conflict over the specifics in a game of hopscotch. The interesting thing is that pitch is not something that we consciously think about and produce; indeed, the pitch may give away indications of forms of thinking in our inner voice that we really wanted to keep private. Intonation is a complete bodily manifestation; and yet, it is consistent with other observable behavior that manifests a particular disposition and orientation. Thus, when we do a voice analysis of the speech in Fragment 6.1, we observe steps in pitch between

ARGUMENTATION AND THE THINKING BODY 111

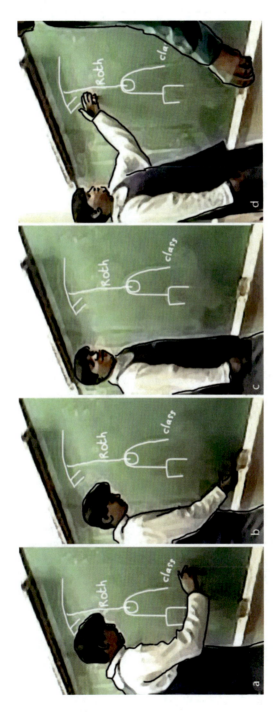

Fig. 7.1 Although there is a continuous movement from finalizing the diagram (a) to laying down the chalk (b) to orienting in the direction of the opponent (c), and back to the diagram again, there are different in-order-to motives in play, none of which can be explained in terms of a composite of body or mind.

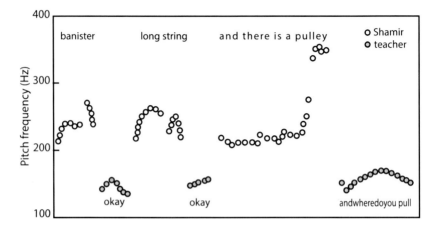

Fig. 7.2 In normal situations where speakers are in agreement and aligned, the pitch levels of the next speaker tend to pick up where the preceding speaker has left off and then return to the second's speaker normal range. The non-aligned pitches manifest the same differences that also manifest themselves in other ways: the different positions that are worked out through scientific argumentation.

consecutive speakers (Fig. 7.2). In the graph, we depict changes in which the pitch of the teacher begins considerably below Shamir, and the pitch in Shamir's voice is considerably above. The pattern also is observable when Shamir says something with a low pitch, which is then followed by something with a much higher pitch. We note that in contrast to the Roth and Tobin and other studies, there is no aggravation of the situation, where the pitches of consecutive speakers continue to rise until reaching three or four times the normal level for a speaker. That is, there is a difference in pitch allowing us to hear the non-alignment while at the same time the situation feels like having some reason to it. The situation is oppositive without the vocal markers of a "heated" debate.

Much of what we do in everyday situations does not have to be represented in consciousness before we do it. This has consequences for theorizing (intelligent) human behavior generally and producing argumentation more specifically. If body positions and actions such as writing and drawing do not exist as conscious plans, then we cannot think of behavior as the result of a conscious mind-brain that directs the organism in every step of the way. This is why Vygotsky (1989) contends that persons control their behavior by stimulating the brain from without; it is not the brain that controls persons' behaviors. There is no doubt that the brain is involved in producing what others see our behavior. But we are concerned here with mind (thought), with consciousness. In this case, therefore, the body acts without the conscious mind telling how to do so and what to do. We therefore observe that we cannot explain a human behavior such as that seen in Fragment 6.1 and in Fig. 7.1 in terms of the mind-brain; and there is no way that we somehow get from the comportment of the biological body to the mind. It is much better to begin with the supposition that there is a larger unit that manifests itself for us, contradictorily, in body and mind; or, in the terms that Spinoza used, body and mind are two attributes of a single substance. In the present situation, we will follow the path of others and refer to this unit as the *thinking body*. In using this term, we encourage readers not to think of this substance as the composition (sum, product) of a body ("wet ware") to which mind is added. This has to be so because "*each attribute of one substance must be conceived through itself*" (Spinoza 2002, p. 221). Whereas some scholars read such propositions as indications of dualism in Spinoza's work, this is not so, for there is only one substance that merely manifests itself in dualistic, mutually exclusive ways. This thinking body is something like a third entity, which is neither body nor thought nor some combination of the two.[2]

The one substance—here referred to as the thinking body—is not that making up the individual person. Spinoza uses terms such as *nature* or *life*. Nature, life, manifests itself in different ways, including thought. But thought in the way we know it is not a property of the individual human being. In the cultural-historical tradition, thought (mind) *is* the ensemble of societal relations. Any such societal relation is not something abstract and metaphysical but always is a "*physical relation between people*" (Vygotsky 1989, p. 56). It is easier to make that step to this view when considering thinking not in terms of things that are somehow in our heads, concepts and frameworks, but in terms of things we do. Then the step becomes easy to think of going from things that we do together to doing these things on our own. The individual *thinking body* therefore is but a manifestation of the collective thinking body, nature as a whole, which includes the human species and its particular ways of relating to one another that include language, gestures, and other things that are generally referred to as "signs."

Body and thought are two attributes of—or two perspectives on, points of view on, or observations of—one *single* object: the thinking body. Because that thinking body is a unity, "it cannot act *on* thought, because its existence as 'thinking' *is* thought" (Il'enkov 1977, p. 34). Instead, the very activity of the body as a whole *is* thinking. This position allows us to understand that the thinking associated with the production of the diagrams produced and visible on the chalkboard (e.g. Fig. 7.1) cannot be reduced to any individual conscious mind or a collection of individual minds the sum or product of which is the conversation and the diagrams. Anything distilled as thought is an abstraction from the event as a whole; and this abstraction is possible only after the event has ended. All the movements that led to a diagram are not spatially expressed changes of some thinking that goes on behind (e.g. in the unconscious) but instead thought exists through those bodily movements. Speaking, the production of recognizable and recognized sound patterns, is but one of those corporeal forms of actions of the thinking body.

Thinking cannot be reduced to the body demarcating the individual person, for the beginnings and endings of the chain that includes the production of lines on the

---

[2] Some readers may be familiar with the popularization of quantum theory in the story of Schrödinger's cat, which, sitting in a box, is going to be killed by a quantum event. At any one point in time, the cat may be alive or dead. The description of the system has the cat both in alive and dead states, which is nonsense. But this description is very different from the actual observation, which turns out either a cat that is alive (analogue to the mind) or a cat that is dead (analogue to the body).

chalkboard and words lie outside the communicating individual (see chapter 2). From a Spinozist point of view, thinking therefore cannot be located in the individual (e.g. Shamir) because the explanation of "thinking" requires the inclusion of the conditions within which the event is born of necessity rather than arising fortuitously. The Spinozist position that Vygotsky was taking toward the end of his life, therefore, radically challenges the constructivist approach for it acknowledges that

> all talk about an idea that first arises and then tries to find material suitable for its incarnation selecting the body of man and his brain as the most suitable and malleable material, all talk of thought first arising and then "being embodied in words," in "terms" and "statements," all such talk, therefore, from Spinoza's point of view, is simply senseless. (Il'enkov 1977, p. 44)

In the Marxian Spinozist approach that was coming to Vygotsky during his last days, we may think of the relation of body and thought in terms of the analogy of an organ and the function that it performs. If the body is the organ and thought is its function, then it becomes immediately apparent that a description of the structure of the body does not yield its function, and the description of its function does not describe its structure. In other words, we cannot conclude from analyzing the structure of something how it is going to be used: a stone may be used as a hammer to crack nuts or as a bullet to be thrown to kill a bird. The same material body (e.g. sound-word) may have different functions (e.g. question, statement, evaluation), and different material forms may realize the same function. To understand thinking as the function of an organ (i.e. the body),

> it is necessary to go beyond the bounds of considering what goes on inside the thinking body, and how (whether it is the human brain or the human being as a whole who possesses this brain is a matter of indifference), and to examine the real system within which this function is performed, i.e. the system of relations *"thinking body and its object."* ... Thought can therefore only be understood through the investigation of its mode of action in the system thinking body–nature as a whole. (Il'enkov 1977, p. 52)

As a result, thought is characteristic of the system as a whole rather than of the single individual body or in an interacting collection thereof. That lesson, in the particular form that it unfolds, in the back and forth of the event that has Shamir talk and the teacher with others as witness, is part of the collective work realized to make this recognizably a science lesson. This sense is inscribed in the situation as a whole so that every one can witness it as something that is common sense: "Of course this is a science lesson, this is why we do all of this." Therefore, "in the ideas that we have of the external world, two quite dissimilar things are muddled and mixed up: the form of our own body and the form of the bodies outside it" (p. 67). We already have expressed this in chapter 2, where we note that speaking, which is addressing itself to the other, for whose benefit it is, takes this other into account. Speaking therefore includes aspects that are characteristic of the speaker while also including aspects characteristic of the other and of the common situation and in-order-to motive that they inherently share. Shamir and the teacher share their common orientation to the in-order-to motive, establishing the warrant for the claim that the teacher could have the banister without winning the tug of war. This particular motive is embedded in the encompassing one of realizing a science lesson, which realizes the science course. But science is only one of the school subjects that have Shamir enrolled within the societally motive of schooling. To understand the event of thinking, we cannot but take into account all of these levels. If there had been a tug of war outside of the school—e.g. involving Shamir's dad, on the one side, and the son with a bunch of neighborhood kids on the other side—then we would have observed something entirely different and would have come to different conclusions about thinking, knowledge, and other related topics that science education researchers of formal and informal science are interested in.

In the Marxian Spinozist approach, there is no doubt that there are things happening in the head. What we grasp as our thoughts is enabled by the grey matter of which consists the specifically human structure of the brain; and there is no doubt about the psychological existence of inner speech. But the subject is not in the head but exists outside of it, in the world, characterized by a condition of *being-in-the-world*; the subject therefore "is something quite other than the *internal state of thought, ideas,* the *brain, speech, etc.*" (Il'enkov 1977, p. 20). Others concur, for example, in stating that "consciousness ... must be located in the objective world rather than in the brain—it belongs to, or is a characteristic of the environment in which we find ourselves" (Mead 1972, p. 112). Being in the world means being in the real affairs of our mundane life; and it means competently acting in situations, which refers us to practical knowing-how. There is a huge literature on the difference between knowing a theoretical discourse *about* something and knowing how to appropriately act in the never-repeating, once-occurrent world in relation to this something. Just as the thinking that we might attribute to Shamir really begins and ends outside of him, so does that which we might attribute to the teacher. Indeed, their thinking coincides in as far as it manifests itself in the situation (their mutual orientation), the words they exchange (hear and say), the images on the chalkboard, the prosody, the gestures, and so forth. All are manifestations of a joint, social activity and process, argumentation and its parts, which, as "acceptance or nonacceptance, rebellion or reconciliation—now become the basic categories for thinking about the world" (Bakhtin 1984, p. 78). Thinking fundamentally is dialogical, which first exists as a social relation and then comes to exist in the behavior of the individual, who takes on and addresses all the roles that previously are played by the different actors in the drama of social life.

Thinking and Speech

The psychophysical (body–mind) problem was a major concern for Vygotsky throughout his scholarly life; but the problem was accentuated near the end of his life when he realized that his own theory focusing on "meaning" was much too intellectualist and thus biased toward the mind. On a library card dating to 1932—

i.e. around two years before his death—Vygotsky notes that the "nub of the question of the spiritual and the material in human consciousness" consists "not in the relation between the brain and the psyche" "but in the relation between thinking and speech, in which the latter is its materialization, its objectivization, its embodiment, a <u>continuous</u> transition of the external to the internal and the internal to the external, a real rather than imaginary unity and struggle of opposites" (Vygotsky 2010, p. 94). On the same card, he refers to a statement by Karl Marx from *The German Ideology* (Marx and Engels 1978), which, at the time of Vygotsky writing, has had its first ever publication (in Moscow and in German). In the statement to which Vygotsky refers, Marx asserts the curse of the materiality of consciousness. Vygotsky actually quotes Marx in the original version of *Thinking and Speech*, but all English translations subsequently simply omitted the quotation. Thinking and speech are articulated as the central problem and as the high road [*via regia*] to historical psychology, that is, to the solution of the body–mind split that has dominated philosophy and psychology since Descartes. At the end of the fifth library card made available to the public, Vygotsky returns to Marx, paraphrasing the statement relating consciousness and speech: "the curse of matter on pure consciousness is moving layers of air, i.e., intercourse with the aid of language, rather than a connection with the brain! *Sehr wichtig* [very important]!" (Vygotsky 2010, p. 95).

Vygotsky never could develop these ideas. This is apparent from the fact that they entered his last completed, posthumously published *Thinking and Speech*. They entered this work not in its body but in the final parts that he wrote: the last paragraphs of the book and parts of the introduction. In the last three paragraphs, Vygotsky outlines the future prospects of his work. What he presented in *Thinking and Speech* only brought him to the threshold of the problem of consciousness, which he deemed to be even more profound than the problem of thinking. The text states,: "*thinking and speech are the key to understanding the nature of human consciousness*" (Vygotsky 1987, p. 285); and he uses several quotations from *The German Ideology*, which, because it had not been available before, he could have read only recently. In these quotations, Marx notes that (a) language is consciousness for others, and thus consciousness for the self; (b) consciousness is cursed with materiality (rather than being something metaphysical); and (c) language is as old as consciousness. Every word, indeed every sign that appears in the exchange between Shamir and his teacher and witnessed by everyone else present in the classroom is a manifestation of consciousness in and of that situation.

Vygotsky points out that the word must be considered as a manifestation of consciousness that exists for two or it does not exist at all. This is one of the findings that we present in chapter 2, and which we present again in Fragment 7.1.

Fragment 7.1
```
4  S:   (says) <long string>
4  T:   (hears) <long string>        5 T: (says) okay
```

If the "lo*ng* str*ing*" did not exist for the teacher, then there would be a disconnect between the two speakers, they would be speaking past each other and thus not have a relation at all—were it not for all the other surrounding aspects that they produce together. We do know that two persons may be close, talking, but not be in a relation with another at all, each speaking for itself.

In the debate concerning the tug of war, no such talking past each other is apparent. Participants may not understand one another, but this sense of not understanding itself is a manifestation that they communicate but not in intelligible way. The conversation is treated as having the underlying intent to be intelligible. Fragment 7.1 makes intelligible that the opposition observed between the speakers also exists within the speakers: in the form of the contrast between the pitch of the incoming "lo*ng* str*ing*" and the outgoing "okay" (Fig. 7.2). That is, the situation inside reflects the public situation, and the public situation reflects the inside situation. The two situations actually are the same, aspects of the same situation artificially divided into an inside and outside. Just as it appears in the preceding quotation, there is a continuous transition of the external to the internal and from the internal to the external. These continuous transitions not only exist for all participants, but, in their communication, they overlap, as seen in the fragment. It is therefore that Vygotsky asks us to engage in a deterministic analysis of psychical life, that is, to investigate thinking where it has its beginning and its ending; and these precisely are not found *within* the individual. Thus, a deterministic analysis of psychical life cannot begin with an ascription of thought to some magical internal power; it is impossible to "determine behavior through one of the individual's own inner systems" (Vygotsky 1987, p. 50). But it is equally impossible to grasp behavior without considering thinking, treating it as a mere appendage of observable behavior.

From these considerations, it is clear that the transition between outer and inner—between physical and intellectual—is that which we call mind so that the physical is inseparable from the psychical (mental). It is not surprising then to find Vygotsky (1987) writing about a vital process "that involves the birth of thought in the word" (p. 284). Returning to the analogy used above, we may consider speech to be the organ and thinking one of its functions (another being a means for social exchange). Inner speech, inner dialogue, is build on external speech, external dialogue. We do not need anything stored inside the head, or have some mental structure that serves as a memory for language and speech. Instead, in the Spinozist approach,

> the organ of thought, while remaining wholly corporeal and therefore incapable of having schemes of its present and future actions *ready-made* and *innate within it* together with its bodily-organised structure, [i]s capable of actively building them anew each time in accordance with the forms and arrangements of the "external things." (Il'enkov 1977, pp. 50–51)

In speaking, we can then produce thoughts even though we have never thought or constructed these before—which is the antithesis to the theses of the constructivist approach. In speaking we not only manifest familiarity and knowledgeability but also generativity but also generate thought.

Vygotsky (1987) recognizes that the interfunctional relations and connections are inaccessible to the old psychology, including scientific (physiological) and interpretative psychology. A real grasp of these interfunctional relations is possible only when research analysis is conducted in terms of units, one of which is the unity/identity of thinking and speech. We thus must not reduce Shamir's body movements (e.g. those that produce sounds) and gestures to mental structures and constructions, just as we must not attempt to explain his conscious awareness in terms of physiology. That is, appropriate analytic units include the intellectual, affective, and practical dimensions of behavior, each taken on its own irreducible to any other modality—just in the way that Marxian Spinozist approach would have it. Each modality is only a manifestation of that complete unit, the *thinking body*, of which the individual human body is but one of the pieces of the entire puzzle.

Investigating the relationship between thinking and speech has become the high (regal) road to the psychophysical problem in the work of the later Vygotsky because in the word manifests itself not only intellect (thought) but also affect. This is perhaps unsurprising because some psychological research provides evidence for considerable correlations between (a) speech parameters, such as intensity, pitch, pitch contour, higher order frequencies (technical referred to as F1 and F2), and (b) lived and felt emotions. Thus, the above-presented pitch differences and the nonalignment of adjoining pitches (Fig. 7.2) are manifestations of the affective orientation that appears when we engage in a competition with someone else. Here it is to be emphasized that Vygotsky does not accept talk about affect in lieu of affect, for talk is characteristic of the social and already represents concepts and interpretation, which is very different from the physiological states and changes that we actually feel. We feel our blushing rather than interpreting a bodily state as shame-associated blushing. It is precisely when we are in synchrony with one or more others that we feel good, where being in sync manifests itself in the pitch (intonation) synchrony, whereas anger and conflict manifest themselves in strongly contrasting pitch levels and contours. Vygotsky therefore suggests the existence of a dynamic sense-giving system—perhaps sometime later he might have written a dynamic sense-giving—that constitutes a unity/identity of the affective and intellectual aspects of being.

Unity/Identity of Body and Mind

The very notion of *argumentation*, with its association to the mundane expression of having a (verbal) argument, all too easily lends itself to a constructivist approach and the reduction of knowing to the mind-brain. In the analysis of the episode involving Shamir and his teacher, we show how the bodily (hand/arm gestures, body orientation to recipients, prosody) events are part of a larger event that also includes speech. All the different communicative modalities are but manifestations of a single unit; but this unit cannot be reduced an intellectualist "meaning" associated with the conceptual content (dictionary sense) of a word. There are studies that show how communicative performances change when students repeat them (Roth 2015). In such situations, the relative amount of communication in the different modalities changes from demonstrative movements, to symbolic gestures, and eventually—especially when testing situations are involved—to the verbal mode. A hand gesture cannot ever turn into a word; it is never the same as a word (or any other sign for that matter) because of the ontological difference (see chapter 6) between any two given signs. The relation between the different forms that communication takes in the course of development is to be found within the unity/identity of an every-changing thinking body. In the Marxian Spinozist approach that Vygotsky was taken near the end of his life, gestures (as other body movements) and words are of a different kind: the latter cannot replace the former. There is therefore no relation of cause and effect "between thought and body ... but the relation of an organ ... to the mode of its own action" (Il'enkov 1977, p. 34).

In the approach that we advocate here—which can be found in the Marxian Spinozist and in the phenomenological scholarly traditions—the body does not need (mental) schemata of its present or future action to be capable to move in patterned ways that are appropriate to a given situation. It is for this reason that thinking is appropriate in the contexture of a (material and social) reality outside of the body. In fact, what is reality and where to draw the boundaries between inside and outside is itself the product of a continuous coming and going (cf. Dewey and Bentley 1949/1999). Shamir's hand/arm movements and vocal gestures are appropriate to the situation at hand because they have arisen from, and are consistent with, the structures of the inscriptions that are evolving on the chalk board. The same can be said of the bodily movements and vocal gestures of the teacher. We therefore must go beyond the confines of the individual body and brain case and consider the thinking body as a whole. We note above that this thinking body exists in social life-as-event in its entirety, and each thinking body of the individual person is but one part of this whole. As in the case of all other part–whole relations, the part cannot be understood outside its relation to all other parts that make the whole, so that the whole is reflected in all of its parts. It might have just been a realization of this kind that led Vygotsky to write that the sense of a word depends on the understanding of the world as a whole. The (sound-) word cannot be reduced to dictionary sense ("meaning") because, as we quote Vygotsky in chapter 1, has absorbed its intellectual affective content from the whole situation in which the word is a constitutive part. That is, the (sound-) word mobilized in the course of an argumentation is a synecdoche, a part reflecting the whole that it also contributes to constituting. The word, thus, "is a microcosm of consciousness, related to consciousness like a living cell is related to an organism, like an atom is related to the cosmos" (Vygotsky 1987, p. 285). In the very last phrase of the original *Thinking and Speech,* Vygotsky notes that a word that makes sense constitutes a microcosm of human consciousness, which, as he states in the preceding paragraph, is cursed with materiality and therefore cannot be understood other than through the material (bodily) aspects of life.

In his earlier work, Vygotsky distinguishes the higher psychological functions from the lower (biological) functions. The lower functions constitute the biological roots and organic properties of the former whereas the higher functions have their basis in real human relations. Although this distinction between the two types of function is considered to be one of the pinnacles of his work, Vygotsky himself is critical of this position, as shown in a note that he made during a symposium 18 months before his death:

> The higher and lower functions are not constructed in two tiers: their number and names do not match. But our previous understanding does not [work], either: a higher function is the mastering of a lower one (voluntary attention is the subordination to oneself of involuntary attention), because this does mean two tiers. (Vygotsky, in Zavershneva 2010, p. 72)

That is, Vygotsky treats this distinction between the lower and higher function as a reincarnation of the psychophysical problem and the Cartesian dualism between body and mind.

Science education researchers interested in learning and development during preschool and the early school years, therefore, *must* account for the biological/bodily as well rather than focusing solely on non- (meta-) physical ideas attributed to the words. We must not reduce argumentation and the development of related competencies to the use of words and phrases in a particular (Toulmin argumentation) pattern. The metaphysical "meanings" are typical of "interpretive psychology," which holds that "mind is primary" (Vygotsky 1997b, p. 12). Because this interpretative approach seeks to theorize human development "hidden behind words" it fails to distinguish between "the biological and the cultural in psychology of child development" (p. 12). The whole of development is reduced to and disappears in the mind, which constructs itself and the world in the process of autopoiesis.

In the take of the later Vygotsky, to understand children's development with respect to argumentation, we need to take into account the bodily and psychological changes, which are but manifestation of the changes of a unitary being. The two "orders of changes mutually penetrate each other and form in essence *a single order of social-biological formation* of the child personality" (Vygotsky 1997b, p. 20). The bodily (non-verbal) and intellectual (verbal) aspects of communicative development are not different modalities or developments on different planes but mere reflections of a single moving and developing system.

We know where Vygotsky was heading, for only a month prior to his death he had given a lecture in which he proposed a new category and an associated unit of analysis. He called it *perezhivanie* (Vygotskij 2001), a word that translates into English as experience or feeling, and which some translators render as emotional experience. However, Vygotsky used this Russian word to render the German terms *Erlebnis/Erleben*, which, though often translated as "experience," really refer to the ways in which we live through and witness (not grasp) what is happening from within, as it is happening and without our knowing what ultimately will have happened. *Perezhivanie* is presented as the unity/identity of person and (material, social) environment. The pertinence of this category to our analysis of the lesson fragments is apparent because we make explicit the irreducible relation between the physical environment (e.g. the form of the inscriptions and the respective positions that the two main actors have with respect to each other) and the communicative performances. Communication is a constitutive part of the event, which therefore cannot be reduced to person and environment. We show how speech and gestures are comprehensible only when considered in their relation to the physical and social environment in the narrower sense of the classroom event as much as in the wider sense of the science lesson (event) within schooling at large (event). In chapter 6, we do show the constitutive relation that exists between verbal and gestural deixis and certain aspects of the physical environment, which become part of the accented visible. Words specifically and communication more generally establish and organize the social relation; and they make sense precisely because of the social relation that they contribute to establishing. The pertinence of the category is shown above in the examples that show how an appropriate theory of thinking needs to take into account the environment, which provides the departure and the end point of the event of thinking.

Students, teachers, and others participate in argumentation in view of the reigning situated in-order-to motive. Any thinking, affect, sensation, and perception is inextricably situated in, reflective of, and affecting the environment—all these modes of being are manifestations of the same unit/identity constituted by the thinking body. To understand the learning and development that occurs in lessons such as those that we analyze above, categories and smallest units of analysis are required that retain the phenomenon as a whole. Argumentation generally, and the production of claims or warrants specifically, cannot be understood through the verbal mode alone. We do need to understand the motive of the activity, which reflects itself in the position (orientation) Shamir has taken, physically, affectively, practically, and intellectually, with respect to the tug of war, the alternative outcome, and the struggle between the different positions in supporting an alternative claim.

Perezhivanie captures the unity/identity of the biological body, the material and social setting, and the overall event (activity) that has practical, intellectual, and affective dimensions. Importantly, we cannot get from the different manifestations—i.e. from thinking, affect, sensation, and perception—to the whole, perezhivanie. Instead, "in perezhivanie we are always dealing with an irreducible unity/identity of characteristics of personality and characteristics of the situation, presented in experience" (Vygotskij 2001, p. 76). As a result, in considering behavior, such as the different contributions students make in argumentation, the environment cannot be identified independent of the contributing person, and the contributing person cannot be understood independent of the environment. This is so because an understanding of the role of relevant individual characteristics in performance requires a thorough description (knowledge) of the environmental characteristics; and understanding the role of the environmental on performance requires a thorough description (knowledge) of the person characteristics. All of these characteristics include affective, intellectual, and practical aspects. We thereby advocate an expansion of research on argumentation to include aspects that go beyond the confines of the dictionary sense of the words and phrases students use, and goes beyond the (non-) compliance of the phrases with some predefined (Toulmin argumentation) pattern.

On Overcoming the Psychophysical Problem

In this chapter, we present an approach intended toward overcoming, theoretically and methodologically, the traditional body (outside)–mind (inside) dichotomy that also characterizes the constructivist approach in science education generally. We make a case for the Marxian Spinozist approach that the late Vygotsky has been taken. In this approach, the bodily-material-physical and the psychological (mental) are but different, contradictory manifestations of one and the same substance. Only a few years after Vygotsky, Freud, whose theories intellectualized the psyche, comments on the extended (physical) nature of his research object: "the psyche is extended, does not know thereof" (Freud 1999, p. 152). That is, the human mind (psyche) is body, and that fact is exactly what escapes the mind (human psyche) in the constructivist approach. In the late works of both scholars, therefore, the dichotomy of body and mind has been overcome, replaced by the unity/identity of one substance.

The Marxian Spinozist one-substance approach that Vygotsky advocates during the later years of his life has considerable consequences for theory and method in science education research. Science education, because of its historical interest in hands-on activity and conceptual understanding, is a prime field of research for advancing the Spinozist approach. In rejecting studies that are but intellectualistic theories, Vygotsky might well have pointed to studies on conceptions or discourse in which the material physical aspects of learning and development have disappeared. In his position there is a bi-conditionality in the development of tool use and the development of body movement and perception. The respective developmental processes—one related to the physical body, the other to the psyche—are manifestation of one process of development in which the bodily and psychological are but (one-sided) manifestations. Just as Vygotsky proposes to study the development of speech comparatively in deaf and normally hearing children, where equivalent problems arise at very different biological age, science educators might want to engage in comparative study of the development of scientific discourse when children and youths have extensive practical engagement with natural phenomena versus when they only talk about such phenomena. This would then allow unpacking the inner relation between the material bases of discursive understanding. With Vygotsky, we might quote Marx on the material course of discourse and discursive understanding. Science educators thereby would develop a better empirical evidence and understanding for how the manual-practical aspects of doing science are related to the conceptual-discursive aspects.

In this approach, mind is not different from the body: body and mind (psyche) are but two manifestations of one and the same thing inaccessible in itself: the thinking body. This approach, opposed to Cartesian dualism and the various forms of body–mind parallelism that reproduce dualism in new guises, requires theorizing a number of pairs of exclusive oppositions as contradictory manifestations of the same phenomenon that has an inner unity/identity. From the perspective that Vygotsky was taking, the contradictions do not arise because of the different perspectives that can be taken on some phenomenon but because of the non-self-identity of the phenomenon. This non-self-identity is the direct consequence of life as a moving phenomenon, so that all psychological phenomena—e.g., speaking and thinking—need to be understood as events manifesting the overarching life process. These manifestations cannot be understood on their own, as if they were elements that could be theorized independently and be put together to form the whole unit. Instead, proper psychological analysis needs to identity the smallest units that retain all the properties of the whole. It is illegitimate, therefore, to theorize speaking (discourse) independently of speaking and thinking, person and environment, individual subjectivity and collective subjectivity, or the biological body and psychological life. It would equally be illegitimate to simply conflate the two members of a pair. Theoretically, the units are denoted by means of *categories*. Each category reflects a minimal unit of the material ever-changing life of society, which is conceived in terms of the relations with others. A category does not denote a thing but something moving, leading to a process description of events and development rather than to a description in terms of differences between two points (things).

References

Bakhtin, M. M. (1984). *Problems of Dostoevsky's poetics*. Austin, TX: University of Texas Press.

Dewey, J., & Bentley, A. F. (1999). Knowing and the known. In R. Handy & E. E. Hardwood (Eds.), *Useful procedures of inquiry* (pp. 97–209). Great Barrington, MA: Behavioral Research Council. (First published in 1949)

Freud, S. (1999). *Gesammelte Werke band XVII* [Collected works Vol. 17]. Frankfurt/M: Fischer-Verlag.

Il'enkov, E. (1977). *Dialectical logic: Essays in its history and theory*. Moscow: Progress.

Marx, K., & Engels, F. (1978). *Werke band 3* [Works Vol. 3]. Berlin: Dietz.

Mead, G. H. (1972). *Mind, self, and society: From the standpoint of a social behaviorist*. Chicago, IL: University of Chicago Press.

Mikhailov, F. T. (2001). The "other within" for the psychologist. *Journal of Russian and East European Psychology, 39*(1), 6–31.

Roth, W.-M. (2015). The emergence of signs in hands-on science. In P. Trifonas (Ed.), *International handbook of semiotics* (pp. 1271–1289). Dordrecht: Springer.

Roth, W.-M., & Lawless, D. (2002). When up is down and down is up: Body orientation, proximity and gestures as resources for listeners. *Language in Society, 31*, 1–28.

8

Teaching Argumentation in Elementary Science

In chapters 2 through 7, we develop a perspective on argumentation in elementary science classrooms that differs from the (social) constructivist perspective that currently reigns the literature in the field. Our perspective is built on some ideas that occurred to the well-known Russian psychologist L. S. Vygotsky very late in his life. At that stage, he was critical of and abandoned the intellectualist approach that he had taken throughout his career; and he moved to an integrated approach where there was a unity/identity of person and environment in experience (pe-rezhivanie). In this chapter, we articulate some ideas about how teachers might act such as to assist the birth of argumentation practices in their science classrooms.

To promote argumentation-based science teaching, requires enhancing teachers' argumentation practices and their intellectual grasp of its educational purpose; and it also requires conditions in which teachers' roles as agents are enhanced allowing them to create argumentation practice in classrooms (Ibraim and Justi 2016; Simon et al. 2006). In many studies of argumentation in science classrooms, much emphasis is given to the structure or elements of arguments in student talk or writing to understand the levels of students' argumentation. Teaching argumentation in classrooms has been understood and practiced as helping students accomplish a specific structure of argument rather than argumentation. In classroom practice, argument and argumentation have been used interchangeably, yet the two need to be rethought in terms of teaching goals and approaches in classrooms. Argument is a product or manifestation of argumentation that focuses on the presence and format of certain features in written or verbal statement whereas argumentation is a sequence or exchange of arguments which shows how cognitive and social interactions take place to solve problems in the community (Andrews 2010). Students learn to participate in argumentation by formatting arguments with certain elements at individual levels, but they need to get engaged in social interactions to learn argumentation as a process. We specifically show that students participate in argumentation even though they may not produce all steps on their own. Indeed, argumentation exists in and *as* the social exchange relation produced in part by their classroom talk. Classroom practice and studies of students' argumentation in existing studies have been argument-based rather than focusing on argumentation-based instructions, by highlighting structural elements of arguments in students' work. As shown in the preceding chapters, argumentation is a process of thinking body as a whole to think and experience. The thinking body manifests itself in different modalities (e.g. speaking, gesturing, moving body) so that the social nature of argumentation cannot be revealed and understood merely through the analysis of the verbal or written products of argumentation events.

When teachers understand argumentation as argument, their teaching practice tends to be structural rather than dialogical. They then tend to want to teach the grammar of argumentation rather than argumentation as event. The structural approach focuses on teaching the elements and structures of arguments such as how arguments are structured with certain elements (e.g. claims, data, warrants, rebuttals, etc.) and how those elements are connected in an argument to become justifiable and convincing. This structural approach is often practiced with emphasis on students' writing practice of arguments. Researchers using this approach often conclude that young students' cognitive abilities are insufficient for participating in argumentation practice. They thus tend to teach argumentation patterns only later in students' lives (e.g. in high school). But if this take on developing a practice were correct, then we would never allow toddlers to babble just because they do not yet master speaking and because they do not yet know the grammar. Thus, classroom practice often focuses on argument-focused instruction to prepare elementary students to be ready for argumentation. Yet if the purpose of teaching argumentation is to develop students' scientific reasoning and problem solving skills, teachers' approach to argumentation needs to be readjusted to go beyond the acquisition of structural arguments. Their teaching would need to look more into how ideas are shared, evaluated, critiqued, and developed through social relations with materials and other bodies to move forward the present problem-solving event.

Our research suggests that it may be more useful to invite young students in debates over science-related issues and then to show them parts of the structure. That is, rather than teaching structure first and then try engaging students in argumentation is at the opposite pole of engaging students in interesting issues that are contested and then use their own discussions as the object for reflecting on the parts of an argument. Music educators discuss similar issues, where some favor teaching solfeggio before allowing students to play the instrument of their choice. Others, such as the Suzuki method for teaching violin, instead have children actually play to learn playing the instrument much in the same way that we learn a first language (where learning the grammar follows knowing the language). Much as young children easily learn a second language and often speak them like their mother tongue, having young children engage in debate from which argument structures evolve may be more suited to develop this aspect of science in schools.

Argumentation as social event precedes arguments as products in classrooms. We may thus introduce argumentation in the early elementary school grades. When argumentation-based instruction is practiced in elementary classrooms allowing children to engage each other and teachers in a dialogical manner, teachers may then participate in classroom conversations as facilitators and members of a problem-solving community. Throughout dialogical argumentation-based classroom practice, teachers are positioned to pay more attention to the epistemic standards of scientific reasoning—e.g. the roles of evidence and claim evaluation in students' problem solving and provide appropriate scaffolding. As participants while children are exchanging, teachers are provided with some extra time for looking in situ not only at the nature of the arguments that emerge but also how arguments are developed through the exchanges and how those (materials, inscriptions, bodily expressions, etc.) move forward in the public forum the ideas and problem-based reasoning. As we show in the preceding chapters, argumentation emerges and develops while students are engaging each other, while working on problems using physical objects, signs, bodily touch and gestures, etc. Once argumentation emerges with these encounters in classrooms, teachers can then contribute to argumentation throughout dialogical problem solving process. Looking into pedagogical actions demonstrated by the teachers in one of our studies, this chapter discusses teaching for argumentation-based instruction in elementary science classrooms.

Attending to the Physicality of Argumentation

In the preceding chapters, we show how classroom materials become the center of thinking and acting in classroom activities. During the activity of mystery object and floating soaps, thinking, dialogues, and actions were oriented and developed around the materials provided for classroom activities. The mystery object, "onion-looking tulip bulb" (chapter 3) raised much challenge and questions on what it is and how to evaluate claims and evidence among all participants (i.e. children and the teacher). The mysterious nature was already embodied in tulip bulbs, which look like onions but not onions. The object itself was giving enough potential to develop reasoning process in this classroom from the immediate perception based on prior knowledge and observation to reflective inquiry with further investigation on evidence, which developed the emergence of argumentative discourse. The two soaps (chapter 5) were also at the center of the collective (including the teacher) reasoning on floatability and buoyancy, revealing experiences and understandings of the common sense features and deviations thereof of physical objects in water. When the two soaps were acting against commonsense experience, the classroom talk was characterized by statements of wondering, questioning, and explaining the deviation of soaps in the water at the scene. To make sense of the conflict between the ideal soap (sinking in water) and the acting soap in front of them (floating in water), question–answer sequences focused on why the white soap floated and the orange soap sank. Other materials such as marbles and ping-pong balls did not show further discussion whereas the two soaps became objects of surprise, question, and discussion. These objects were inseparable from the observed, inherently public thinking and reasoning processes. This example showed certain physical objects were more likely to develop argumentation discourse in classrooms than others (i.e. those materials that were known and behaved according to commonsense experience). The onion-looking tulip bulbs and the floating soaps were going beyond the intuitive forms of reasoning that played themselves out in the public forum. When physical objects embody certain deviations from the commonness of ideal objects, there exist possibilities for developing reflective thinking and argumentative discourse to understand why the object is not acting ideal in that case. That is, the emergence of reasoning and argumentation was already embedded and immanent in the materials, tulip bulbs and floating soaps. In our study, it was evident that children actively responded to the materials and the potential of argumentative discourse was embedded in the materials. As the materials played important roles to develop classroom dialogues, actions, and reasoning, teachers' awareness and decision making on classroom materials may play an important role. Providing materials of potential conflicts is an effective way of scaffolding children's reasoning and argumentation.

Another layer of the physicality of reasoning and argumentation is that children's thinking and speaking is not only mental and verbal but also bodily and multimodal. Seen in chapters 6 and 7, reasoning and argumentation were expressed through multiple modalities, including inscriptions, gestures, prosody, etc. Thinking presented itself in bodily expressions, which words alone could not explain. The verbally stated claims that the discussion over the tug of war allowed to come forth from Shamir's mouth (chapter 6 and 7) initially did not make sense to other participants (classmates and teacher like). But thinking became intelligible when in additional body movements over and about the drawings on the chalkboard came into play. The drawings on the chalkboard and bodily engagement such as pointing on the drawings were part of the argument communicated in that instant. The physical components of argument and argumentation make something non-intelligible intelligible for words to make sense in classroom talk. Reasoning and argumentation cannot be reduced to verbal and mental process or products as the engagement and expression of the physical body are unavoidable parts of thinking and speaking. Learners as a unity/identity of social, physical and psychological beings continuously are one with the environment so that any thinking and acting was changed simultaneously. Teachers therefore need to pay attention to the possibilities of the physical nature of children's reasoning in classrooms.

As classroom materials change, thinking and talking also change. The conflicts, doubts, and wonders embedded in materials have potential to emerge and orient reflective reasoning and argumentation, as these play themselves out and are accessible in the public forum of the classroom talk. In this regard, reasoning and argumentation is *material*. Reasoning and argumentation is also *physical* for bodies thinking, experiencing, and making sense of the context in the course of claim making and justifying. They physicality of reasoning and argumentation needs to be rethought and examined in classrooms as argumentation has been regarded as children's verbal and written products of claim-evidence justification. This contrasts the constructivist approach where teaching practices heretofore tended to focus on children's linguistic performance and reasoning as mental process. Sharing more examples and research findings on reasoning and argumentation as physical and material, there needs to encourage teachers to pay more attention to contributing to the conditions such that multimodal learning and communicating events are enhanced to improve scientific reasoning and argumentation-based problem solving.

Pointing and Formulating

Pedagogically, pointing at an action or moment and framing it with certain meanings and values can be a useful contribution to teach children new and abstract conceptual and material practices. For instance, a mother is trying to teach her child the virtue of "sharing." The child has not developed what has to be done so that the action deserves "sharing" as an appropriate description. When her child is playing with a friend, the mother gives one of her child's toys to the friend and says, "Let's share your toy with her." The action of handing a toy to a friend is formulated as "sharing." From a pragmatic linguistic perspective, there is a language-game in play, which may be termed "training" but could just as well be called "educating." Thus, "an important part of the training will consist in the teacher's pointing to the objects, directing the child's attention to them, and at the same time uttering a word" (Wittgenstein 1953/1997, p. 4). In our case, "sharing" is not a tangible thing but a form of event, which the associated talk formulates. When the child is grabbing and giving a cookie to her friend, the mom says "Great! You are sharing a cookie with her. That's good that you share things with friends." The mother formulates (names) the action of giving a cookie, thereby making it an object of reflection, and discusses it in terms of sharing, and frames it as a good thing. The child is hearing the mother formulating the action of giving something to her friend is sharing and sharing is a good thing. (Of course, this requires the competence to understand the talk *as* formulating something that stands out, where it is unclear whether the action does indeed stand out so that the action makes sense *as* "sharing.") The child is educated in the practice of sharing and sharing, as per the evaluative comment, is good. The goodness of sharing is a concept not easy to grasp on the part of a young child, but through the mother's act of formulating and framing, she starts to participate in sharing in a public forum. This is why the early (individualist, cognitivist) Vygotsky (1978) is made to explain—on the part of the editors, who, in their own words, actually concocted the text—that higher cognitive abilities are experienced and developed in interpersonal levels first and internalized in intrapersonal levels later. Nothing really has to be internalized because the child already participates in sharing and in hearing the action formulated.

Argumentation is a complex concept and skill for students to understand and practice in classrooms. Specifically, epistemic standards of argumentation such as the coherence between claim and evidence and importance of evidence in problem solving contexts are more advanced practices that take more experience to be fully mastered. Direct teaching through the structure of arguments would not sufficiently develop the competency of talking in ways such that these epistemic standards can subsequently be isolated from and said to be characteristic of the talk. These have to be experienced, practiced, and recognized in the context of argumentation for students to understand the meanings and importance of epistemic standards in argumentation. The second-/third-class teacher participating in our study demonstrated strategies of pointing and framing to emphasize the importance of claim-evidence relationships in one's justification in her science classroom. She explicitly acknowledged "evidence" in her explanation of certain situations and students' responses and actions during classroom problem solving. The following example shows how she introduced and acknowledged the words, evidence, and conclusion. The teacher and students were reviewing the previous experiment to discuss the function of the cotyledon. The event has the teacher formulate for the children the data observed and recorded as evidence. Based on this evidence, a claim (conclusion) was drawn to explain the function of cotyledon in class.

T: so, the last step of your experiment is. ... we have evidence. we saw that it was shriveled up and when it was all used up it was um ... it fell off the plant so that's some of our evidence, right, we recorded that, and our conclusion is ... so a conclusion is kinda the answer to a question, right? the question was what is the function of a cotyledon? so, I think that the function is to ...

K: give the plant food!

To produce a conclusion to the question, "What is the function of a cotyledon?," the community reviewed the observations made throughout the experiment and the teacher formulated what was said as something having stated the *evidence*. Based on this, a public articulation of the function of cotyledon is born: to give the plant food. The articulation is not the child's own, or something that could be relegated to her brain. Instead, the articulation is born in and out of the talk specifically and all the observation events that happened earlier. Formulating here emphasized the importance of evidence in the making of claims and the associated problem-solving process.

Another example can be seen during the mystery object problem solving (chapter 3). When children voiced claims without accounting for the smell as evidence, the teacher asks them to pay attention to evaluating evidence to justify their claims. The request has its origin in what the children were voicing and, therefore, is not attributable to the teacher alone. When students voice ideas and describe data from observation, and previous experiences to support their claim, a statement emerges that formulates the preceding talk as having stated the evidence ("that's your evidence!"), which is associated with an evaluative commentary: "good that you brought us evidence." The following are specific examples of the ways in which the teacher responded to students during class conversations in order to emphasize the importance of evidence.

- I think that's a good piece of evidence.
- I don't think the evidence supports that it's an onion. So what else could it be?

- What is the evidence that tells you that it's an onion?
- So, you could say, "I think that these pieces give me evidence for why you think it might be a root."

The videotape provides evidence of questions about the visibility (observability) of something that could serve as evidence for making certain claims. The teacher talk included phrases such as "the evidence supports …," "the evidence that tells …," or "give me evidence for why you think" to emphasize the connection between claim and evidence in argumentation. The formulating talk also made note of the quality of evidence, such as the accuracy and amount of evidence ("what really happens," "real evidence," or "good evidence"):

- Do we have enough evidence to really know what this is?
- I don't see a whole lot of evidence here.
- Let's focus on what actually happens.
- We want to be scientists and we want to use real evidence.
- So, if you were going to conclude that it's an onion, you have to give me some good evidence.

Not every idea, observation or datum is good evidence but there is better and stronger evidence than others to justify claims and students need to evaluate the quality of evidence to justify claims in their decision-making.

The emphasis on the importance of evidence by formulating was clear. Students started to show their understandings of strong evidence and making claims based on evidence. The following exchange is from the last class of the mystery object activity. Students explained that smell was good evidence to justify that the object was not garlic.

T: so, we know that with garlic, a big piece of evidence would be what?
C: the stench
K: okay, so what does the evidence tell you?
K: it's not garlic.

Teacher was part of and contributed to the emergence of evidence-based claim making continued throughout the term and helped students provide evidence to explain their claims. Researchers posit that teacher modeling of higher cognitive thinking skills such as scientific reasoning and argumentation is critical for students to learn and practice them in their own discourse (Gillies and Boyle 2005; Yilmaz et al. 2017). The teacher modeled the actions of "seeking and evaluating evidence" in the classroom problem solving with children. Whenever she made the effort and noticed students making that effort, she pointed and framed the moment as evidence-based problem solving.

Being a Member of a Problem-Solving Community

With the expectation and prioritization of content knowledge in the science curriculum, classroom teachers are often positioned as knowledge providers and students as knowledge receiver. In this one-directional relationship of teacher and students, teaching tends to be a script-based performance to achieve the prescribed learning outcomes rather than open improvisational instruction that allows the moments of emergence and creativity of co-constructive knowledge building between teacher and students (Sawyer 2004). Argumentation, often emerging from classroom interactions, requires teachers' attentiveness and flexibility to notice and develop the emerging moment of argumentation. It requires active participation both from teacher and students to experience the importance of epistemic criteria in the dynamics of argumentation. Teachers need to shift their position from knowledge provider to inquirer and problem solver through collective communications and students freely and constructively share their ideas in classroom talk (Mercer 2000).

The teachers in our study played a significant role as members of classroom problem-solving communities to facilitate classroom argumentation. Rather imposing correct knowledge on the mystery object problem solving, she contributed in ways that she hoped would open space for questions, wonders, and doubts to initiate further investigation for learning. Our studies show that argumentation was emerging with these encounters and the teachers positioned themselves as arguers, who were trying to convince others with her evidence. The community members' positions, teacher or student, were mutual and collaborative to solve their classroom problem. The second-/third grade teacher explained that she felt tension when classroom activities were unfolding something different from her curriculum intention. Despite the tension, she did not tell the right answer to the students but played as one of arguers who had a counter claim with different evidence. She said to the students:

> I'm not convinced. to me, it, if the evidence isn't showing me, isn't saying onion because it's not like any ... unless it's a new kind of onion I've never seen. How could we test it? (Excerpt from chapter 3)

Rather than saying "I know it is not onion but tulip bulb" with teacher authority, she formulated the importance of having a convincing evidence in her turn taking. She said that the evidence did not tell her it was onion. At the same time, she did not discard students' claims completely but she opened a possibility that it could be a new kind of onion that she'd never seen before. She acknowledged her experiences could be limited to only a few kinds of onions, thus, not definite to prove this was not onion, and therefore that there was a need for further investigation. This turn led children to evolve test designs to examine the object further. She contributed as a thinker and arguer, who seeks evidence to support claims, evaluates the quality of evidence, and also listens to others' claims and evidence with open-mindedness to participate in conversations. Through this teacher-students relationship, argumentation and knowledge of mystery object emerged and were further developed.

The episodes we feature in this book show that children and their teachers do not always agree. Nor is either party easily convinced by the other—even when it might be assumed that the teacher "knows more." Until there are opportunities to openly examine ideas against other claims and evidence and confirm some claims are not right based on a new set of evidence, it is hard to accept another's idea or grasp the words and phrases offered up as explanations. The authority of teacher as a knowledge holder and giver did not seem to help convince children sufficiently to accept the teacher's claim in. To reconcile the moment of two opposing ideas, the teacher is a member of a dialogical community. They participated in the problem solving process together with the children until a collectively acceptable way was found resolve the conflict. Argumentation evolved in the mutual relationship of problem solvers. Reasoning and problem solving through evidence were experienced and verbalized together with the teacher in classroom talk.

To promote argumentation-based teaching, teachers provide students opportunities to share different ideas, questions, and critiques and open to change their minds based on evidence. Students learn to scrutinize knowledge claims against evidence and negotiate and reconcile the differences and conflicts of knowledge claims to reach out the best solutions. When children are engaged in argumentation-based problem solving, classroom discourse flows into different paths depending on problem contexts, curriculum, materials, and the dynamics of social relations among participants. Sometimes, scientifically correct descriptions are discarded without any further discussions; and sometimes, scientifically wrong descriptions are broadly accepted based on power relationship or friendship in conversations. At times, important ideas are ignored due to the lack of students' interests or relevant experiences. Some problems are too controversial to be reconciled among students and sometimes students do not have enough knowledge to evaluate claims or resources to find evidence for their claims. These various dynamics of learning environments and classroom interactions make students' argumentation complex and unpredictable.

The nature of complexity of learning through classroom interactions is challenging for teachers to scaffold students' argumentation as *process* in classrooms. The path and outcomes of public thinking and acting are emergent, unplanned, and unknown to teachers. This requires teachers' mindful and attentive pedagogical noticing and acting in the situation (where there is no time out for reflection). The teachers in this study were mindful toward how students accept and reject claims and how they reason and evaluate evidence in collective levels. By giving up the authority of knowledge holder and provider, they created dialogical communities of problem solving that gave rise to the development of ideas, questions, and critiques. The teachers could thus be seen as modeling how to evaluate claims and how to respect evidence; they strove to be experienced as contributors to the problem solving process. Argumentation was becoming a process of reasoning and problem solving in a collective learning community. To develop students' reasoning and argumentation skills, it is critical for teachers to create the culture of deliberative collective problem solving where students share and critique ideas freely and constructively. Researchers often state that when students shared the goal of reaching the best answers *together* in argumentation tasks rather than persuading others in a structure of claim vs. counterclaim, students' argumentation becomes more productive and efficient in terms of cognitive and social learning (e.g. Felton et al. 2015). Students with the goal of deliberation for consensus can develop to the point of producing longer exchanges of thoughts by accommodating and expanding others' ideas and providing valid critiques. Thus, there can be more opportunities for further reasoning and learning on curriculum topics in consensus-oriented argumentation rather than persuasion-based debates. In the discourse of deliberative problem solving process, students come to practice respect for others' claims, evidence, critiques, and alternatives to solve the problem. Students also come to grasp and perform argumentation as a form of social relation with others to find answers in collective manners.

To enhance students' critical thinking and decision-making skills for problem solving in future society, students need to learn how to argue with knowledge, skills and respect to differences, alternatives and possibilities. In classrooms as problem solving communities, students are provided opportunities to encounter opposing views, respect evidence rather than opinions, and promote consensus for social cohesion (e.g. Erduran and Kaya 2016). Yet in encountering different or conflicting ideas, students in elementary classrooms are sometimes reluctant to change their claims and accept others' even though they know others' ideas are more convincing. With this attitude, students do not reach a conclusion or consensus among group members. Students need to learn willingness toward negotiating and open-mindedness toward respecting and accepting others' ideas based on strong evidence in argumentation process. Students need to learn that "giving up their own and accepting others' ideas based on evidence" is a virtue, rather than a weakness or failure of argumentation because this means students are capable to evaluate claims against evidence and examine their own misconception. Teachers' explicit pointing and framing this process of "accepting others' claims when stronger and more convincing evidence are provided" as strength and competence would be critical to develop the value of collaborative argumentation. This democratic process of knowledge building and problem solving through argumentation requires teachers to understand the goal of teaching argumentation. Teaching argumentation is not only to help students produce logical statements as final products but a process of problem solving in a community where members share, discuss, and critique to reach out the best solution. This requires a shift of teaching approach from focusing on the structure of argument to understanding the dynamics of reasoning and decision making through argumentation. Argumentation-in-the-making is only experienced, learned, and developed through social interactions and this requires teachers' tactful attention and actions to help students understand and learn how to argue effectively and meaningfully as future problem solvers in society.

References

Andrews, R. (2010). *Argumentation in higher education*. New York, NY: Routledge.
Erduran, S., & Kaya, E. (2016). Scientific argumentation and deliberative democracy: An incompatible mix in school science? *Theory into Practice, 55*(4), 302–310.
Felton, M., Garcia-Mila, M., Villarroel, C., & Gilabert, S. (2015). Arguing collaboratively: Argumentative discourse types and their potential for knowledge building. *British Journal of Educational Psychology, 85*(3), 372–386.
Gillies, R. M., & Boyle, M. (2005). Teachers' scaffolding behaviours during cooperative learning. *Asia-Pacific Journal of Teacher Education, 33*(3), 243–259.
Ibraim, S., & Justi, R. (2016). Teachers' knowledge in argumentation: Contributions from an explicit teaching in an initial teacher education programme. *International Journal of Science Education, 38*(12), 1996–2025.
Mercer, N. (2000). *Words and minds: How we use language to think together*. London: Routledge.
Sawyer, K. (2004). Creative teaching: Collaborative discussion as disciplined improvisation. *Educational Researcher, 33*(2), 12–20.
Simon, S., Erduran, S., & Osborne, J. (2006). Learning to reach argumentation: Research and development in the science classroom. *International Journal of Science Education, 28*(2), 235–260.
Wittgenstein, L. (1997). *Philosophische Untersuchungen/Philosophical investigations* (2nd ed.). Oxford: Blackwell. (First published in 1953)
Yilmaz, Y., Cakiroglu, J., Ertepinar, H., & Erduran, S. (2017). The pedagogy of argumentation in science education: Science teachers' instructional practices. *International Journal of Science Education, 39*(11), 1443–1464.

Index

A

Abstraction, 87, 100, 113
Arguers, 2, 132
Argument, vii, viii, 1–3, 5–14, 16, 22, 25, 27, 30, 32, 37, 43, 44, 47, 48, 53, 58, 60, 63, 65–67, 73–77, 79, 80, 84, 90, 92, 95, 99, 100, 102, 104, 105, 107, 109, 110, 112, 115, 118–121, 125–129, 131–135
Argument elements, 5, 9
Argument patterns, viii, 126
Argumentation, vii, viii, 1–3, 5–14, 16, 22, 25, 27, 30, 32, 43, 48, 53, 58, 60, 65–67, 73–77, 79, 80, 84, 90, 92, 95, 99, 102, 104, 105, 109, 110, 112, 115, 118–121, 125–129, 131–135
Argumentation schemes, viii, 6–9, 14
Attending to, 5, 19, 20, 23, 30, 32, 72
Attentiveness, 132

B

Banister, 24, 26–29, 31–34, 93–95, 98, 100–104, 115
Bodily, 27, 108, 110, 113, 118–120, 122, 127, 128
Body, 10, 12, 16, 27, 28, 66, 100, 103, 107, 108, 110–114, 116, 118–123, 126, 128

Buoyancy, 81, 83, 85–87, 127

C

Chalkboard, 12, 24, 26, 28, 30, 91–93, 98, 100, 101, 103–105, 109, 110, 113–115, 128
Claim, viii, 1–3, 5–9, 14, 38–48, 50, 51, 53–55, 65, 66, 73–77, 79–83, 85–89, 92, 93, 95–99, 101, 102, 107, 109, 110, 115, 121, 126–134
Claim making, 4, 51, 77, 79, 83, 84, 89, 128, 131
Co-construct, 11, 132
Coding, 4, 5
Collective, 5, 11, 30, 32, 41, 44–46, 51–55, 57, 58, 64, 67, 72, 73, 77, 78, 84, 90, 108, 113, 114, 123, 127, 132, 133
Commonness, 83, 84, 85, 89, 128
Configuration, 17, 25, 27, 95, 96, 98–102, 104, 105, 107
Consciousness, 18, 19, 21–23, 32, 34, 35, 51, 63, 64, 76, 77, 102, 107, 108, 110, 112, 115, 116, 119
Constructivism, 1, 10, 12, 14, 16, 17, 21, 44, 45, 57, 59, 67, 71, 84, 91, 95, 109, 114, 117, 118, 122, 125, 128

138 INDEX

Contradiction, 16, 29, 31, 45–48, 61–63, 65, 68, 69, 71–73, 75, 77, 78, 80, 83
Corresponding, 19, 59, 62, 63, 77
Counter claim, 2, 3, 5, 8, 73, 86, 87, 132
Covariation, 2, 8, 38, 43, 44, 88, 129
Critical question, 6–9
Cultural-historical, 10, 30, 35, 56, 77, 84, 109, 113
Curriculum, 1, 9, 10, 39, 40, 45, 48, 51, 55, 79, 80, 90, 96, 108, 132–134

D

Data, vii, viii, 1, 3, 5, 8, 11, 17, 38, 44, 45, 75, 79, 87, 89, 96, 109, 126, 130
Descartes, R., 10, 15, 108, 116, 120, 123
Deviation, 83, 85, 89, 127
Diagram, 12, 91–95, 98–105, 109, 111, 113
Dialogical, vii, 5, 6, 9, 20, 32, 48, 50, 51, 62, 63, 73, 75, 77, 115, 126, 127, 133
Dialogue, vii, viii, 7, 8, 14, 19, 20, 33, 40, 43, 48, 51, 63, 77, 83, 88, 117
Difference, 26, 44, 64, 80, 86, 89, 91, 112, 115, 119

E

Elementary, vii, viii, 5, 10, 12, 13, 17, 44, 58, 59, 66, 77, 90, 92, 109, 125, 126, 134
Emergence, 11, 12, 19, 39, 55, 58, 60, 62–64, 75, 77–80, 84, 123, 127, 131, 132
Evidence, 1–3, 5–9, 11, 13, 14, 19, 38, 40, 43–55, 65–67, 73–75, 77–79, 82, 83, 86, 88, 89, 92, 95, 107, 118, 123, 127, 129–134

F

Facilitation, 132
Flexibility, 132
Floatability, 72, 81, 83–89, 127
Formulation, 31, 32, 47, 66, 75, 129, 131
Framing, 13, 129, 130, 134
Fundamental, 2, 6, 28, 66, 88, 90, 99, 108

G

Gesture, 11, 27, 58, 101, 102, 104, 105, 108, 119

I

Ideal, 8, 24, 84, 85, 86, 127
Improvisational instruction, 132
Initiation-Reply-Evaluation, 18
In-order-to, 24, 31–34, 98, 102, 110, 111, 114, 121
Inscription, 12, 91, 99– 105, 110, 114
Intersubjectivity, 57, 68

J

Joint, 43, 44, 46, 50, 51
Joint social action, 71, 77
Justification, 1–3, 9, 42, 44, 50, 128, 130

K

Knowledge providers, 132
Knowledge receivers, 132
Knowledgeability, 118

M

Marx, K., vii, 15, 16, 18, 19, 35, 59, 87, 90, 114–116, 118, 119, 122, 123
Material, 19, 79, 81, 83, 84, 87, 90, 91, 98, 108, 109, 114, 116, 119, 121–123, 128, 129
Meaning, 10, 17, 19, 22, 23, 25–27, 34, 69, 89, 102, 115, 119
Mind, viii, 1, 10, 12, 16, 18, 21, 53, 54, 63, 71, 91, 107–109, 111–113, 115, 117, 120, 122, 123
Modalities, 119, 120, 126, 128
Modeling, 14, 131, 133
Mutual, 72, 90, 115, 132, 133
Mutually, 23, 27, 28, 62, 102–105
Mystery object, 39, 40, 42–46, 48, 50–52, 54, 79, 127, 130–133

N

Negotiation, 8, 51, 54, 55, 79, 80, 84, 88, 133

O

Orientation, 102

P

Perezhivanie, 120, 121, 125
Performance, 2, 54, 88, 94, 95, 101–105, 107, 109, 119, 121, 128, 132
Persuasion, 8
Phenomenological, 22, 119
Physical, 11, 28, 58, 79–81, 83–91, 103, 104, 113, 117, 120–122, 127, 128
Physical objects, 11, 79–81, 83–90, 127
Pointing, 11, 27, 28, 31, 46, 58, 90, 100–103, 105, 128–130, 134
Practical work, 4, 13, 79, 90
Problem solver, 55, 132–134
Problem solving, viii, 1, 5, 6, 8, 11, 12, 38, 39, 41, 44–46, 48, 50–52, 54, 55, 80, 84, 86–88, 126, 127, 129–134
Prosody, 78, 108, 115, 118, 124, 128
Pulley, 24, 26–28, 30, 31, 93, 94, 96–105, 107, 109

R

Reasoning, vii, viii, 1, 2, 5, 6, 8–14, 16, 17, 37–46, 50–56, 58, 59, 67, 77–80, 83–85, 87–89, 126–128, 131, 133, 134
Rebuttal, 2, 3, 5, 9, 98, 101, 105, 126
Receiving, 19–21, 30, 71
Representation, 91, 99, 100
Responding, 20, 41, 59, 62–64, 70–73, 77

S

Scaffolding, 127, 128
Schütz, A., 22, 23, 33, 35
Sense, 1, 12, 21–25, 27–34, 37, 39, 40, 42, 43, 46, 50–52, 54, 55, 58, 60, 70–73, 76, 77, 85, 87–90, 100–105, 108, 110, 114, 117, 119, 121, 122, 127, 128, 129
Sense-giving, 22–24, 27, 28, 30, 38, 43, 51, 52, 55, 68, 84, 88, 102–104, 108, 118
Sense-making, 52

Sign, 7, 22, 24, 28, 34, 52, 58, 103, 108, 116, 119
Social relation, vii, 10, 11, 43, 50, 51, 53, 57, 58, 75, 83, 109, 115, 121, 126, 133, 134
Speech, vii, 18–23, 27, 28, 30, 33, 35, 58, 63, 64, 66–69, 72, 76, 82, 83, 88, 95, 103, 107, 108, 110, 115–119, 121, 122
Spinoza, B., vii, 11, 12, 15, 16, 58, 107, 108, 113–115, 117–119, 122, 124

T

Thinking body, 16, 108, 113, 114, 118, 119, 121, 123, 126
Transaction, 19, 20, 32, 63, 77
Translocution, 19, 71, 72, 75, 78
Tug of war, 12, 24–27, 31, 92, 95, 96, 98, 99, 101–105, 107, 109, 115, 117, 121, 128

U

Unity/identity, 12, 58, 62, 73, 76, 104, 107, 109, 118, 119, 121–123, 125, 128

V

Vygotsky, L. S., vii, 10–12, 14–16, 18, 19, 21–24, 26, 28–30, 34, 35, 51–53, 57–59, 62, 65, 66, 71, 76, 78, 84, 90, 103, 107–109, 112–120, 122–125, 129

W

Walton, D., viii, 6–9, 14
Warrant, 2, 3, 5, 9, 96–99, 101, 102, 104, 105, 107, 109, 115, 121, 126
Word, 12, 17–19, 21–25, 28, 29, 32–34, 40, 51, 52, 57–59, 62, 66, 68–70, 72, 76, 84, 98, 101–103, 105, 108, 116–120, 129

Printed in the United States
By Bookmasters